ONLY

LIGHTS

Editor-in-Chief
ALEJANDRO ASENSIO

Subeditor and texts
EVA MARÍN

Art Editor
MIREIA FABREGAS

Editorial Staff
MARC GRAU
ROBERTA VELLINI
XAVIER ROSELLÓ
CARLOS RIVERO

Photographic Documentation
SEAN ROVIRA
ASTRID MARTEEN
DANIEL JARAMILLO

Production Director
JUANJO RODRÍGUEZ NOVEL

Design and Layout
MANEL PERET
JORDI CALLEJA

Infographics
TONI LLADÓ FERNÀNDEZ
ENRIC NAVARRO
MANEL PERET

Traduction
MARK HOLLOWAY
MARGARIDA RIBEIRO
DAVID SUTCLIFFE

Copyright © 2004 Atrium Group
Published by:
Atrium Group de ediciones y publicaciones S.L.
Ganduxer, 112
08022 Barcelona

Tel: +34 932 540 099
Fax: +34 932 118 139
e-mail: atrium@atriumgroup.org
www.atriumbooks.com

ISBN: 84-96099-51-2
D.L.: B-50.161-2004

Printed in Spain
Ferré Olsina S.A.

INDEX

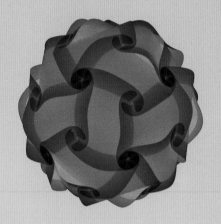

10 WHEN WE DESIGN
A SPACE, WHETHER IT IS FOR LIVING IN OR
FOR WORK, IT IS ESSENTIAL TO CHOOSE THE
TYPE OF ILLUMINATION ACCORDING TO THE
FUNCTION OF EACH AREA.

ceiling lamps

88 ARE USED AS MUCH
to provide overall illumination as for areas in
which particular activities such as reading or
sewing are carried out.

standard lamps

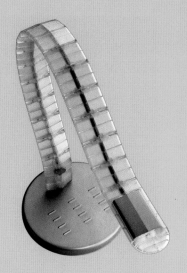

154 FROM ANCIENT

TIMES, HUMAN BEINGS HAVE DESIRED TO
CONTINUE THEIR TASKS AFTER SUNSET.

table lamps

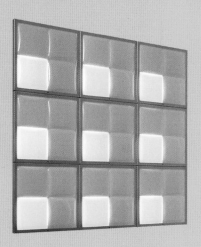

232 ARE FREQUENTLY

USE DTO ILLUMINATE TRANSIT AREAS
SUCH AS PASSAGES, HALLS AND LANDINGS.
THEY ARE ALSO THE ETERNAL COMPA-
NIONS OF BATHROOM MIRRORS.

wall lamps

262 THE LAMPS

IN THIS SECTION, A SERIES OF LAMPS DE-
SIGNED FOR THE EXTERIOR HAVE BEEN
BROUGHT TOGETHER.

exterior lamps

General introduction

S If with the different pieces of furnishings we give body to the places we inhabit and we determine their movement and activity and, then, with the fabrics and accessories we dress them, the lighting is, without a doubt, the spirit of our spaces. Not only does it illuminate the atmosphere, but it also illuminates our interior world. It modifies our perception of what surrounds us and of our very own lives as well. Lighting has two aspects: science and art. In domestic surroundings, the second aspect prevails over the first. We forget about concepts such as quantity of lights or sources and we concentrate more on creating a climate that manages to satisfy our spirit and that provides us with wellbeing. In order to achieve this, there has to be a balance between the entrance of natural light and the amount of the artificial light distributed within the general illumination, the working area, light used to accentuate and that which is decorative. In the different sections of this book, we will become acquainted with the latest proposals that have been made in each of these areas not only by the large firms, but by the sector's smaller manufacturers as well. We will become familiar with the top designers in the field and also with those who are less well known, but who offer their small beams of light to the international panorama of the lamp. In this macro-showcase of the sector, we will come into contact with the latest tendencies that are marked by minimalism for the office and by soft forms and colors for the home. From poetical pieces, and those with a touch of humor, to re-editions of models that have become cult objects, avant-garde lamps, neoclassical lamps, in this book there is room for everything from the most functional designs to the most daring. As Virgilio said centuries ago, "good fortune accompanies the daring."

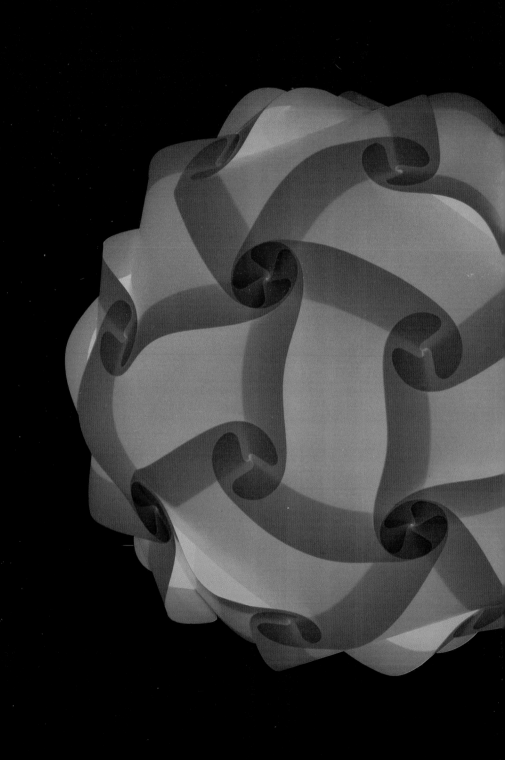

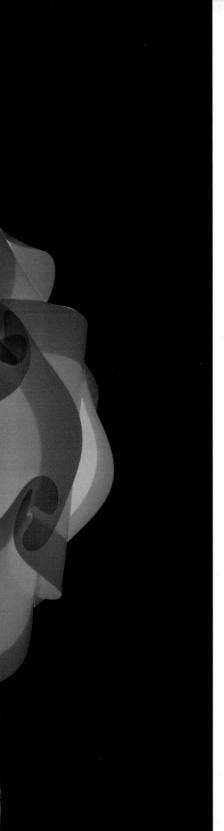

ceiling lamps

When we design a space, whether it is for living in or for work, it is essential to choose the type of illumination according to the function of each area. The two fundamental aspects to bear in mind are the desired atmosphere and the activities which are to be developed in each zone. Hanging lamps are the key elements for general illumination. They reach a large part of the overall volume of the room. They tend to be used over dining room or kitchen tables and in saloons. It is advisable to bear in mind that they create a source of light that, depending on the type of shade and the height at which it is hung, may be more or less intense. However, whatever the case should be they will produce a play of light and shade that should be complemented with other lamps to achieve an optimum atmosphere.

Within this category in this section, we will find a large variety of models ranging from the most traditional proposals to the most avant-garde such as the designs of KUNDA-LINI. Some are based on the reinterpretation of forms from the past. An example of this is Orientale by Michele De Lucchi who, basing his work on oriental traditions, produces contemporary designs of great beauty. Others are full of poetry. This is the case of Porca Miseria from Ingo Maurer or those which contain a touch of humor such as Strangle Light for Artificial (SCP) or Top Secret (METALARTE). For those who feel nostalgia for the 1970's, KARTELL presents Icon in different colors. There is also room for the most playful of lamps here. Those that are made up like puzzles from L.I.N. in natural materials as well as many more possibilities. There is something for all tastes and styles.

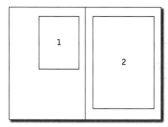

1. Supernova is a design from Ferruccio Laviani for FOSCARINI.

2. Another four versions in white with gray strips of the model IQL LIGHT.

VICO MAGISTRETTI

Profile

Magistretti (1920) is one of those who are responsible for the success of Italian design in the world. Since he began to work in the furniture sector, at the beginning of the 1960's, he has become a maestro of simple elegant lasting forms. He has achieved this without losing touch with popular tastes and the industry and has been able to make the most of all of the advantages offered by the latest technologies. He was one of the first designers to start working with plastics and he managed to change the image that the consumers had of this material: from considering it to be cheap and feeble to seeing it as elegant and sophisticated. In his more than 50 years of professional activitiy, he has received a diversity of prizes among which two Golden Compass Awards (1967 and 1979) can be found. His creations form part of the permanent collection of the MOMA in New York.

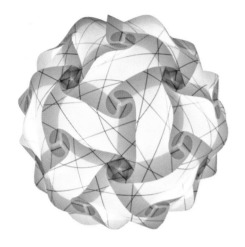

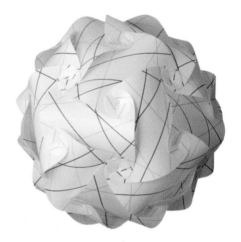

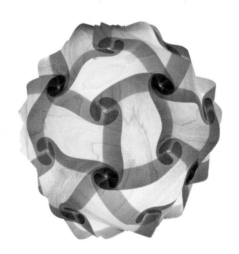

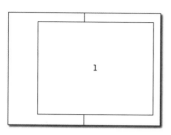

1. Different versions of this model produced by IQL LIGHT and designed by Holger Strom. On the following page, four more proposals from this company.

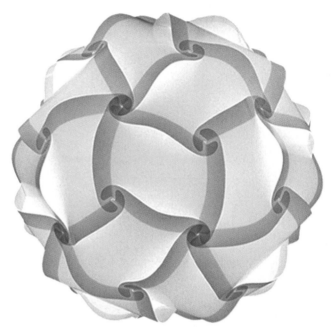

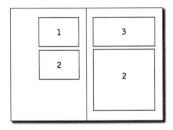

1. SCP include the model 178 from LE KLINT in their catalog.

2. Schlitz Up is a design from INGO MAURER.

3. SKANDIUM propose the model Pend from LE KLINT.

Profile

PATRICIA URQUIOLA

Patricia Urquiola was born in Oviedo (Spain) and she now lives and works in Milan. She assisted Achille Castiglione and Eugenio Bettinelli with the courses that they presented in the Polytechnic Institute of Milan and in the ENSCI in Paris from 1990 to 1992. Later, she started to work for De Padova in the development of new products. She associated with Vico Magestretti and set up a studio. In 1996, she started directing the Lissoni Associati design group for Cappellini, Cassina, Kartell, Artelano y Antares-Flos among others. At the same time, she designed independently for Moroso, Fasem, Livi't, Tronconi and Bosa. She participated in "Abitare il Tempo" from 1998 to 2000 and her products were selected for the Italian Design 2001. She presently has her own studio in Milan and she dedicates her time to design, exhibitions, art direction and architecture.

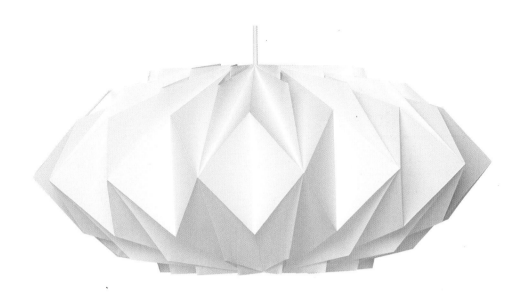

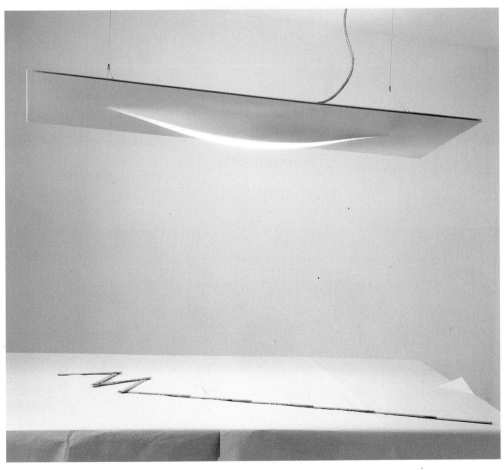

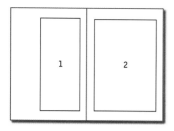

1. De LUCEPLAN, Agave, a design by Diego Rossi and Raffaele Tedesco.

2. Model Airco is a creation from Willem Van der Sluis and Hugo Timmermans for LUCEPLAN.

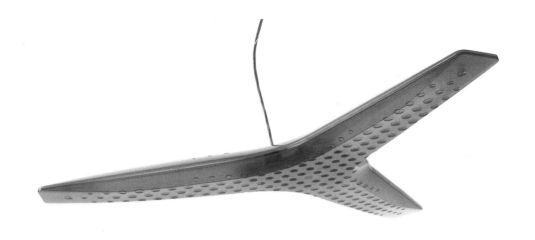

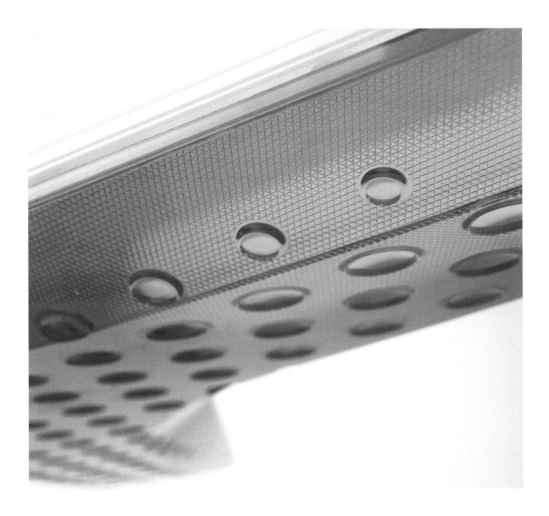

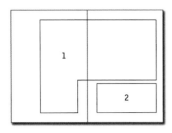

1. From IDL, on both pages: top, Oskar, bottom, other proposals from the same company: Jasmund and Kub.

2. LUCEPLAN produce this design by Jan Ejhed and Aleksandra Stratimirovic: Happy Happy.

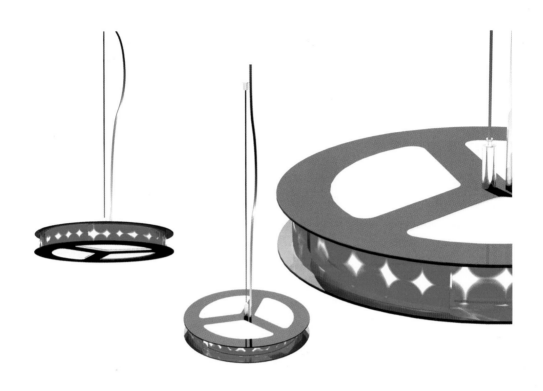

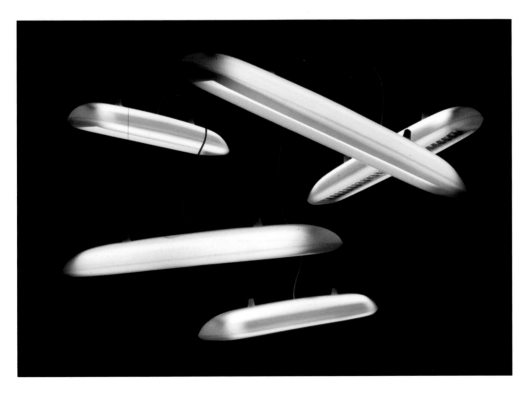

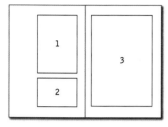

1. From SANTA & COLE's catalog, a design by Antoni Arola: Oven 60, inspired in how light passes through a jellyfish.
2. DAB propose the model No Bu.
3. Lamp produced in different co-lors by MOONLIGHT.

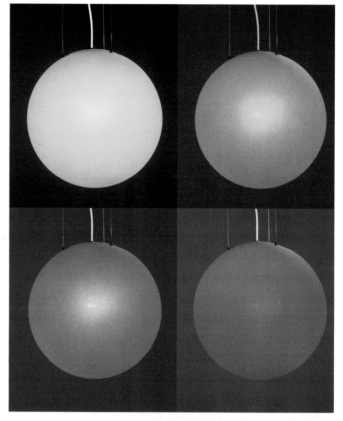

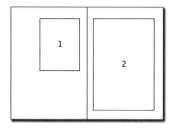

1. Christoph Matthias and Hagen
   Sczech designed Canned Light for
   INGO MAURER.

2. Campari Light is another proposal
   from INGO MAURER created by
   Raffaele Celentano.

INGO MAURER

This German artist has become known by the nickname of "Magician of Light"
or "Poet of Light" and stands out for his creations that contain a very personal
sense of humor. He studied graphic design and worked as a graphic design for
two years in San Francisco and New York. In 1963, he returned to Europe and
settled in Munich. He later set up his own design studio, Design M. For his works
he has received numerous prizes and many of his pieces can be found in museums around the
world such as the celebrated Porca Miseria! (2003) which is included in the Design Collection of the Museum of Modern Art of New York. His lamps have also been exhibited in the
George Pomidou Center and in the Vitra Design Museum (2002) among others. In October
1986, he was given the title "Chevalier de arts et des lettres" by the French minister of culture.

Profile

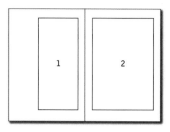

1. ANTHOLOGIE QUARTET commercialize this design by Heiko Bleuel, Light Colors, top, as a ceiling lamp and below as a wall fitting.

2. Icon (Top) and Easy (Bottom) are two designs by Ferruccio Laviani for KARTELL

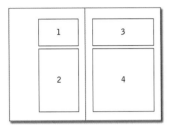

1. Flood is a creation from Hannes Wettstein for the brand PALLU-CO.
2. ELMAR FLÖTOTTO produce the model Pure Glass.
3. The firm ARRMET commercialize Cellu-lite, a model designed by Robby Cantarutti and Claudio Biferali.
4. Minigiò S Rosso belongs to the catalog from MURANODUE, one of FIRME DI VETRO's five brands.

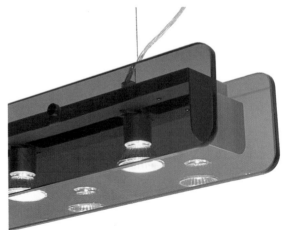

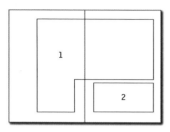

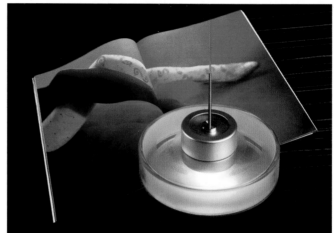

1. Fokus, with clean and pure forms, is a product from BELUX created by Schwarz Späth.

2. Two ceiling lamps from INGO MAURER.

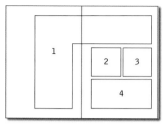

1. On this page, Porca Miseria, a design by INGO MAURER. On the following page, top left and right, another two creations from the German designer.

2. A product from PREALPI available in different colors.

3. Zettelz is a design from INGO MAURER.

4. Chili 2 (flame) is a design from Ayala Serfaty for AQUA CREATIONS.

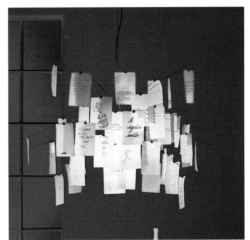
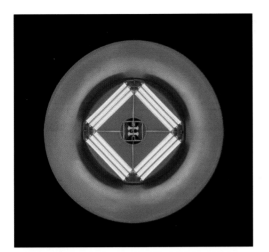

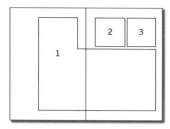

1. Nana Mobile (top, on this page), Stand By (bottom, on both pages) are designs by Ayala Serfaty for AQUA CREATIONS.

2. A design by Emili Padrós and Ana Mir for METALARTE, from the collection Metalab, Colector.

3. Alexander Pernitschka and Mary-Ann Williams from ILLU STRA-TION created Xolo - Flokati Filz.

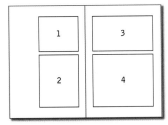

1. B.LUX - VANLUX propose He-
   lios Metal, created by
   M.Ybaguengottia.

2. Model Oval Colgante Wire and
   Flakes Colgante Wire (Bottom)
   from ZLAMP, a proposal from
   SLD.

3. QUASAR present Narita (Left)
   and Fieltebek (Right) designed by
   Jan Pauwels.

4. Top Secret from Héctor Serrano
   belongs to the Colección Metalab
   from METALARTE.

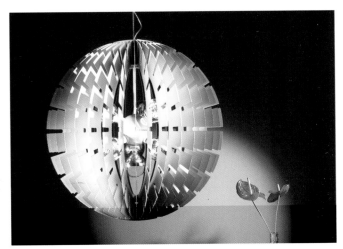

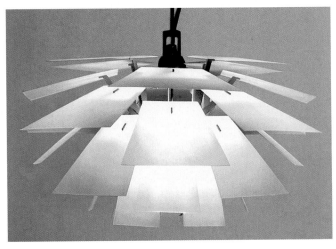

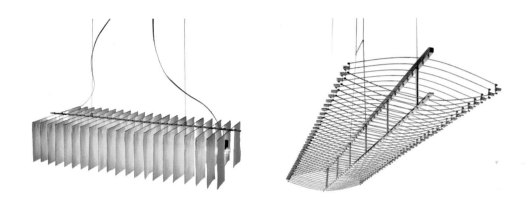

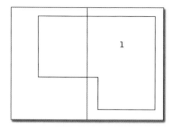

1. Two versions of the model Tubular from the hand of Fabiaan Van Severen and commercialized by DELTALIGHT. Belgian design is starting to stand out for innovative creations which respond to the demands of the public.

ANTONIO CITTERIO

Antonio Citterio (1959) has demonstrated that he has talent in a number of different disciplines. His experience covers a diversity of fields: architecture, interior design, corporate design, industrial design... The furniture of this Italian designer shows the admiration that he feels for minimalist art. As much his architectural creations as his furniture design are characterized by their functionality and they stand out for their essential forms which are able to transmit a lot with very few elements. In order to achieve this expressive simplicity, the quality of the materials used becomes basic. Citterio states that he only designs pieces of furniture that he would like to be surrounded by. His creations can be found in the permanent exhibitions of the MOMA (Museum of Modern Art of New York), the Pompidou Center in Paris and the Museum of Architecture and Design of Chicago.

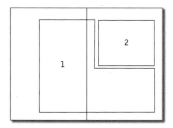

1. One of the lamps from INGO
   MAURER in different colors.
2. A Tool is a design from Christoph
   Matthias for INGO MAURER.

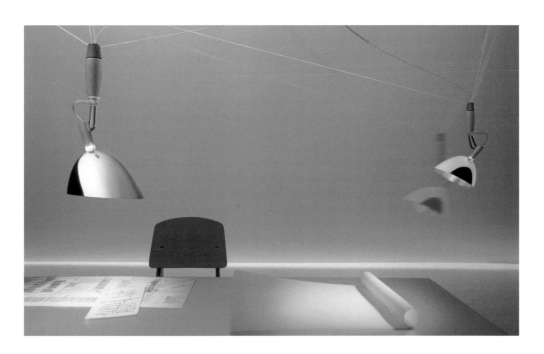

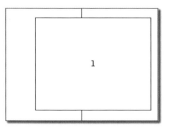

1. Different Models from INGO MAURER. On this page and on the following, top, the XXL Dome. Bottom right, Pierre ou Paul.

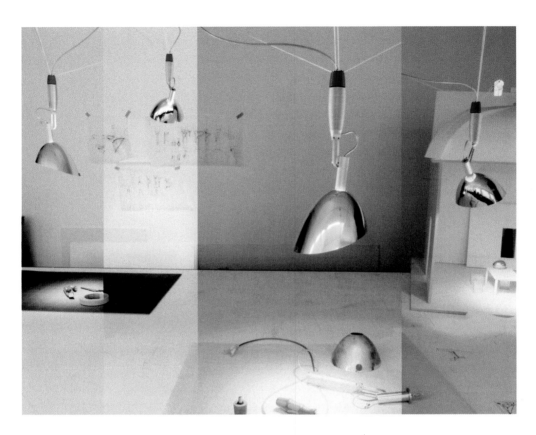

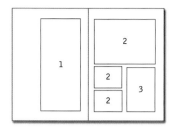

1. On this page, the models Mini Flap System Sospensione designed by Zebulon (Top) and Mini Surf System Sospensione from Neil Poulton (Bottom, left). On the right, a creation from Carlotta de Bevilacqua, Tian Xia. The three lamps are produced by ARTEMIDE.

2. ILUMINACIÓN PETER JAHN propose this design from the brand BERND BEISSE: Beyond. Bottom, the Occhio Ho system from the brand AXELMEISE-LICHT, which also distributes IPJ in Spain.

3. Michele De Lucchi and Gerhard Reichert created Logico for AR-TEMIDE which can be assembled in various three-dimensional combinations and can give direct or indirect lighting.

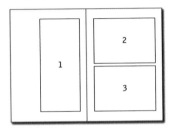

1. From the brand ARTEK, Pendant Lamp A331, created by Alvar Aalto (1953-54).

2. The lamp Faruno-orange from Alex Gabriel & Willeke Evenhuis (RP - LAMPS).

3. VIABIZZUNO commercialize this lamp, H2O, a project from Progetto Letizia Mammini and Mario Nanni.

DENIS SANTACHIARA

Many of the works by Santachiara (1951) lie between art and design. As of 1975 he developed a deep interest in investigation and in new techniques applied to the design of images and objects. The theories and creations that have come out of these processes have been characterized by the way in which they combine magic and technology, multi-functionality and play. For Santachiara there is a fundamental aspect: "I believe that objects should always offer small surprises, something to talk about, that one object should fulfill various functions". His creations are on permanent view in the Museum of Decorative Arts of the Louvre in Paris, the Museum of Modern Art of Tokyo, in the design collection of the Pompidou Center, in the Vitra Design Museum, or in the museums of Lyon and Philadelphia. In 2000, he obtained the Design Word Award in two sections.

Profile

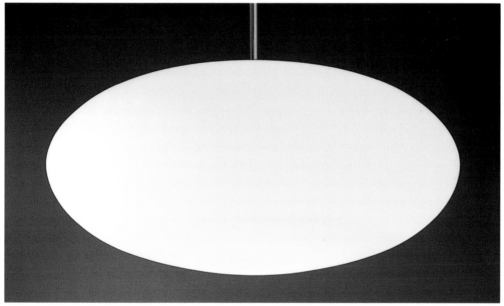

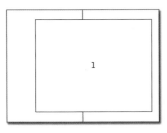

1. Some of the models from the young designers Alex Gabriel and Willeke Evenhuis who make up the team of RP - LAMPS. On this page, from top to bottom, detail of Faruno, Supersigno and Tenilo. On the following page, on the left, Faruno and on the right, top, Tenilo and, bottom, Konko-landscape.

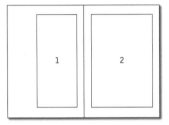

1. Two models from FOSCARINI:
   Lampoon (top), created by Aldo
   Cibic and a design by Rodolfo
   Dordoni, Lumiere (bottom).

2. From RP - LAMPS, Capelo and
   Tenilo (top) and two versions of
   Capelo (bottom) from the crea-
   tors Alex Gabriel and Willeke
   Evenhuis.

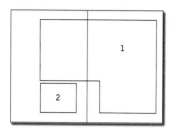

1. FOSCARINI commercialize the models presented on these two pages. On this page: Lampoon de Aldo Cibic. On the following page, Circus (top), a creation from Defne Koz, Cross also from the designer Valerio Bottin (bottom, left) and, to the right, Buds, from the creator Rodolfo Dordoni.

2. Bekkou, as the Japanese creator Kouichi Okamoto is known created Baloon Lamp which is comprises a globe and LED and is commercialized by KYOUEI CO ITD. A low consumption lamp.

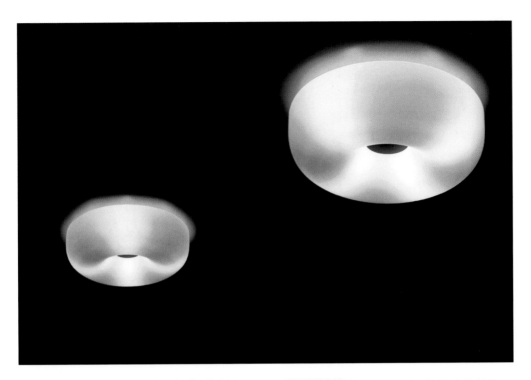

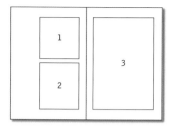

1. On this page, two lamps belonging to the FOSCARINI catalog: Havana by Jozeph Forakis (Top), which is on show in the Museum of Modern Art (MOMA), New York and Dom designed by Roberto and Ludovica Palomba (Bottom).

2. ARTEMIDE present this creation from Michele De Lucchi and Huub Ubbens: Castore.

3. Also from the brand FOSCARINI: Folio (Top, right) and O Space by Luca Nichetto and Giampietro Gai (Bottom).

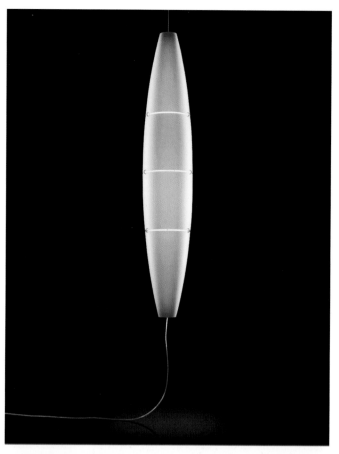

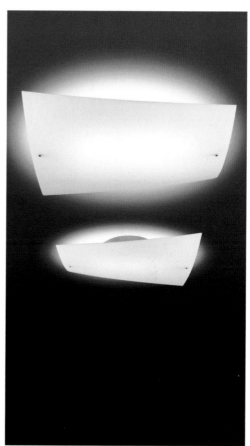

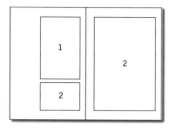

1. Some proposals from LOOKI-LUZ, the models Shikak (Top), Diabol (Bottom).

2. KUNDALINI produce this design by Marzio Rusconi Clerici: Pad-ma in five different colors. On the following page, top, Sama, a creation from Gregorio Spini for KUNDALINI. Bottom, Yu, designed by Marzio Rusconi Clerici, from the same company.

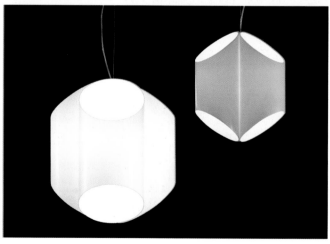

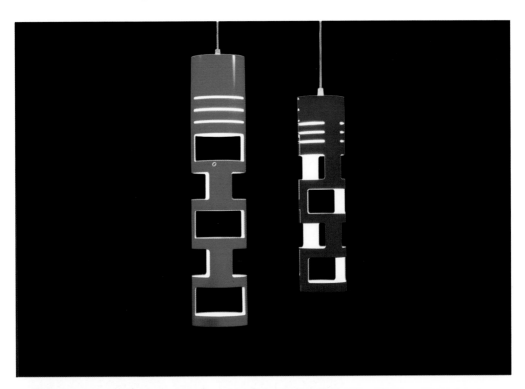

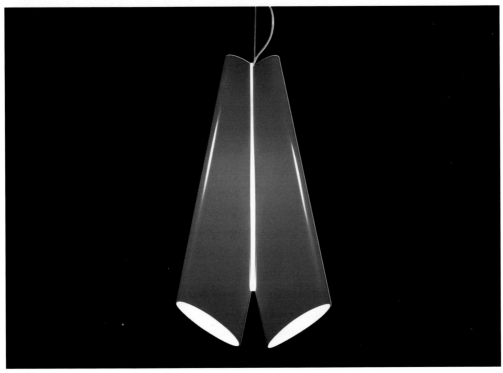

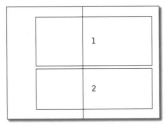

1. DAB propose the model Orange.

2. FOSCARINI produce these designs from Ferruccio Laviani, Supernova (Left); Valerio Bottin, Tutù (Centro); and Marc Sadler's, Tite (Right), which won the "Compasso d'Oro" in 2001.

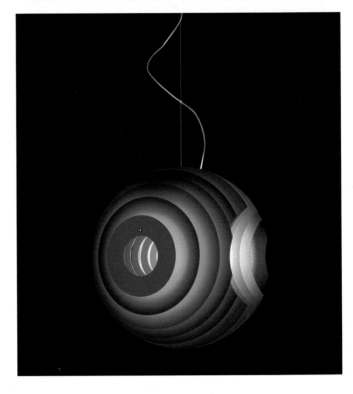

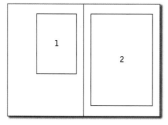

1. ALBUM produce this creation from Design Tanzi, the model Zorro.

2. ILUMINACIÓN PETER JAHN distribute Spiral in Spain, a model from the brand BERND BEISSE.

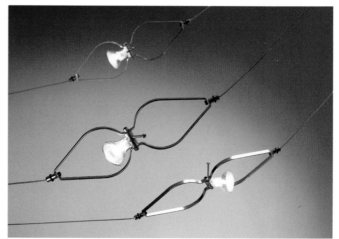

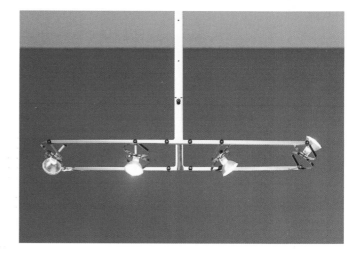

NORMAN FOSTER

Born in Manchester, in 1935, Norman Foster is one of the outstanding architects of our time and representative of what is denominated High Tech architecture. He has been able to apply engineering and high technology to offer innovative architectural solutions to the problems of living places, work places, illumination, furniture and transportation. He has received almost all of the prestigious international architectural prizes among which is found the Pritzker. Among his pieces of High Tech design, he has managed to create an office system of high productivity, the furnishing system Nomos, which has extended to the domestic ambit as a result of its high aesthetic quality and the lighting system for Erco. In both cases, the use of high technology components, the engineering solutions presented and the sense of geometry that they reveal stand out.

Profile

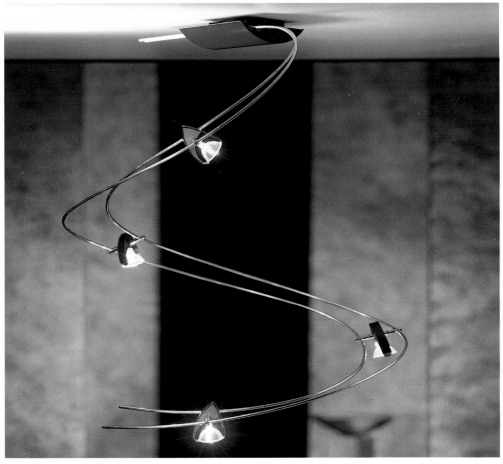

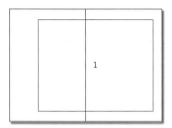

1. From the brand ALBUM the models Fili d'Angelo (on this page), Strale (on the following page, top) and Capalunga (bottom).

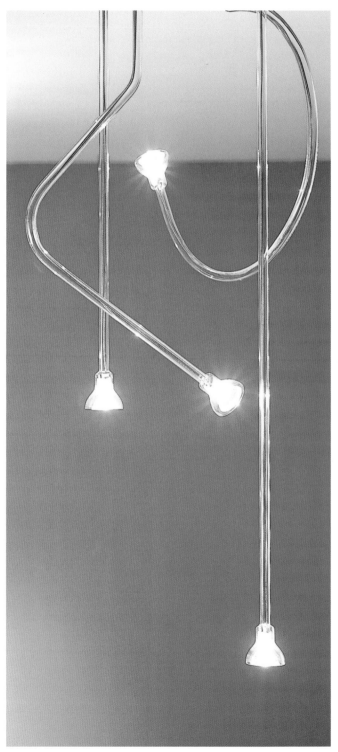

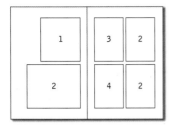

| 1 | 3 | 2 |
| 2 | 4 | 2 |

1. Model RIV from the firm TA-
   LLER UNO.
2. FIRME DI VETRO propose
   Oriente, a model included in the
   ALT LUCIALTERNATIVE catalog.
3. IGUZZINI produce this ceiling
   lamp, Gem.
4. SCP propose this model from the
   brand ARTIFICIAL, Strangle
   Light, a creation from Gitta
   Gschwendtner.

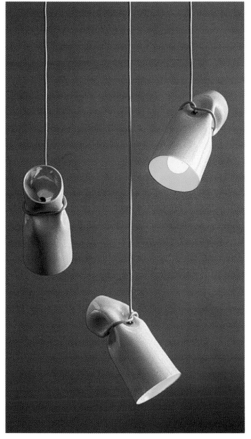

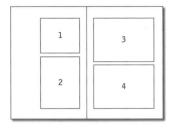

1. LUCITALIA produce this ceiling lamp from Francesco Brivio, Zero.

2. Verform is a producto from L.I.N.

3. B.LUX - VANLUX propose Dolcetta.

4. Blondie Be is a creation in organic forms from AQUA CREATIONS.

1. Two versions of the model Moving from VIBIA.

2. OLIGO propose the model Grace with adjustable height.

3. From the brand IDL, the model Get On.

4. Tulip is a product from VIBIA.

5. Pantalla GT6 is a proposal from SANTA & COLE. This model has been designed for small spaces.

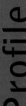

MANEL MOLINA

Manel Molina was born in Barcelona in 1963. He studied interior and industrial design at the EINA School of Barcelona. From 1985 to 1989, he collaborated with Miquel Milà and undertook work in areas such as interior design, refurbishing, temporary exhibition and stand design among others. In 1991, along with Alberto Lievore and Jeannette Altherr he formed the company Lievore Altherr Molina. The studio is presently collaborating on projects in Spain, Germany and Italy among which those in the furnishing sector for companies such as Andreu World; Arper, Casamilano, Foscarini, Halifax, Perobell, Thonet or Santa & Cole particularly stand out. Manel Molina has presented numerous personal exhibitions all over the world and writes for various Spanish and foreign specialized magazines on a regular basis.

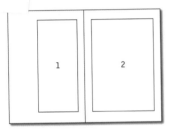

1. Birdie is a creation from INGO MAURER.

2. Lightness, poetry and simplicity are found in T(h)rou(gh), a design by Andrea Anastasio for ARTE-MIDE, of a great sculptural effect.

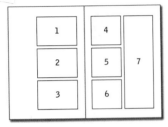

1. A proposal from SCP, the lamp Pendant light no.1, from BODO SPERLEIN.

2. From QUASAR: Universe, a creation from Jan Pauwels.

3. HLF is another proposal from DAB.

4. Gerrit Rietveld designed the model L 40 which is commercialized by TECTA.

5. One of the accessories from the brand CONMOTO.

6. Model Pekin from the brand VIBIA designed by Ramón Benedito.

7. In their catalog QUASAR include the hanging lamps: Bird by Jan Pauwels (top), the model Vicent by Merkx & Girod (center) and Bulb 3 (bottom).

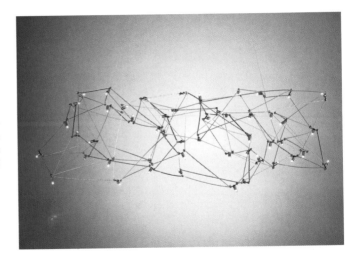

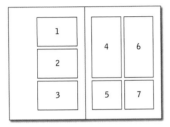

1. The company TECTA propose this design by Florian Borkenhagen: L 60, Saturn.

2. FIRME DI VETRO present the model Angelica Pointer Bianca from the brand ALT LUCIAL-TERNATIVE.

3. Lumiera is a product from AL-BUM.

4. Two versions of the ceiling lamp The Line from the brand QUA-SAR.

5. Trili d´Angelo, a model from AL-BUM.

6. QUASAR present two versions of this creation by Jan Pauwel: Ork Grande. The feathers are optional.

7. Lightweight, by Tom Dixon for FOSCARINI, is a design that oscillates between classical and futurist.

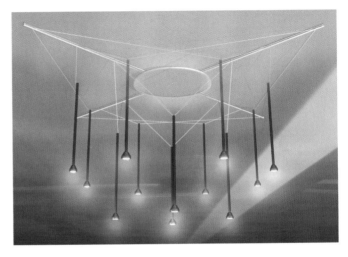

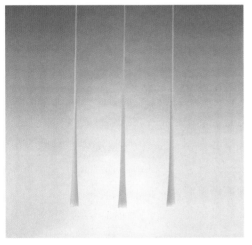

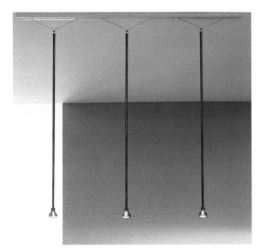

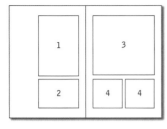

1. The Gasteig of Munich, an emblematic cultural and educative complex in the Bavarian capital, is illuminated with this model. The design was undertaken by Christian Spork from Luxoom GmbH and a specialist from ANSORG.

2. From the FOSCARINI catalog, the model Hola by Roberto and Ludovica Palomba, available in two sizes.

3. Another proposal from FIRME DI VETRO from the brand MURANODUE, the Contessina S3, made from glass blown in.

4. To the left, model Kilocal produced by ALBUM. To the right, Patata, from the same company.

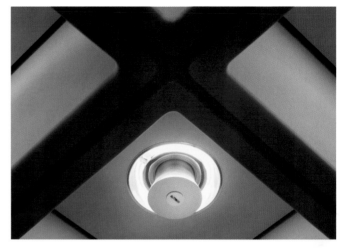

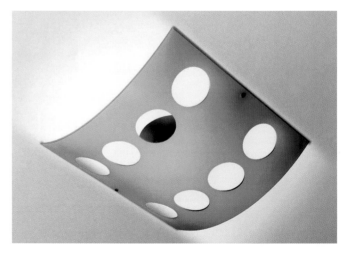

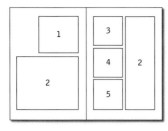

1. A lamp of nautical inspiration from ARTEK.

2. Diverse models distributed by ILUMINACIÓN PETER JAHN from the Occhio collection from the brand AXELMEISELICHT.

3. From the brand CARPYEN, Odyssey designed by Gabriel Teixidó.

4. DAB propose this design by Miguel Ángel Ciganda, the model Zibor QR.

5. Model Paper Soffitto from the brand AURELIANO TOSO of FIRME DI VETRO.

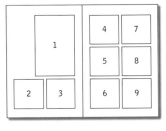

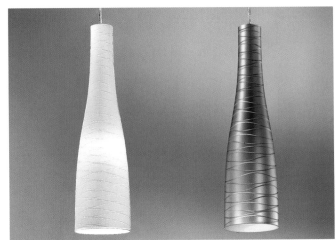

1. FIRME DI VETRO propose Class 40-60 with diffused or direct light, from the ITRE catalog.

2. A model distributed by IPJ, from the brand SCHMITZ-LEUCH-TEN ITZ, Gino.

3. PENTA present Luume, a design by Massimo Belloni.

4. Napoleone belongs to the catalog from VIBIA.

5. Nina is a ceiling lamp commercialized by VIBIA.

6. Another model from QUASAR, Hat.

7. Ceiling lamp from the brand SCHMITZ-LEUCHTEN ITZ, distributed by IPJ in Spain.

8. VINÇON distribute this model from Pellitteri Design, Uno.

9. Alexia is a creation from Álex Soler for CARPYEN with finishes in metallic lead, white and titanium.

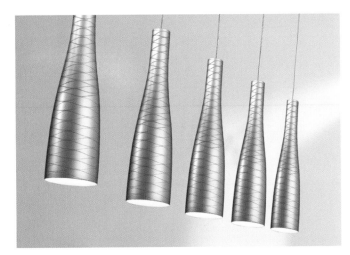

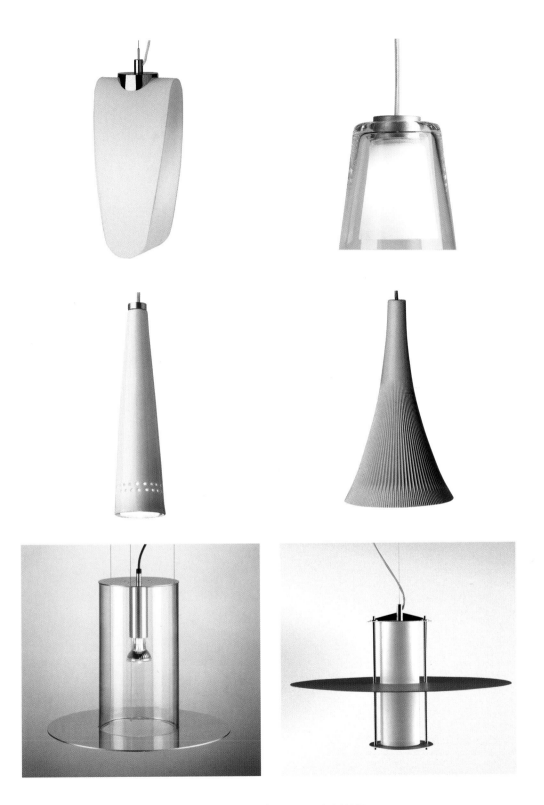

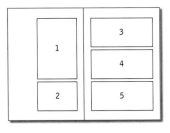

1. Bruno Gecchelin designed Metro (top) and Cerchio (bottom) for IGUZZINI.

2. A ceiling model from the brand OLIGO.

3. Also from the brand DELTA-LIGHT the models Labo Hic-35 AD (left) and Nobody 140 (right).

4. CARPYEN present Focus Mini by Gabriel Teixidó.

5. Another product from DELTA-LIGHT: Labo 2Hic.

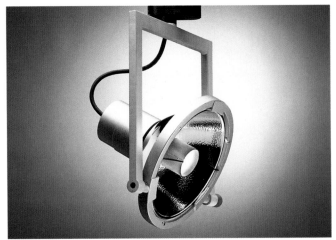

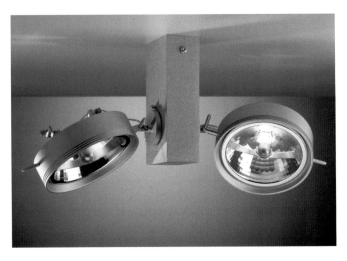

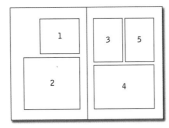

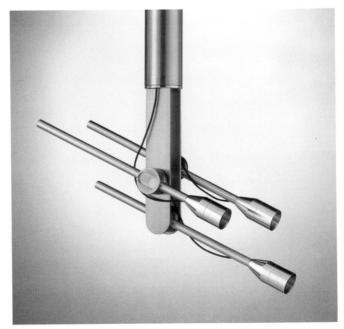

1. QUASAR produced by Miru Spot (top) and Miru XL (bottom) designed by Jos Muller.

2. Joan Gaspar created the Neón Luz for MARSET.

3. In their catalog, CARPYEN include this design by Gabriel Teixidó, Dial.

4. DELTALIGHT propose Limit Trimless.

5. Flash is a design from Gabriel Teixidó from the brand CARPYEN.

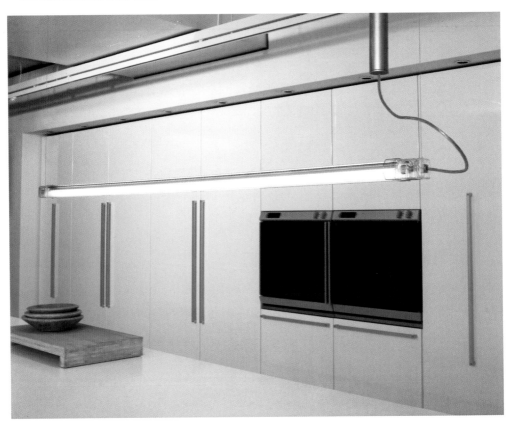

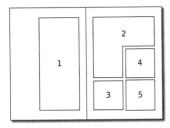

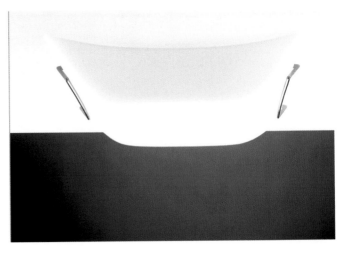

1. CARPYEN present these designs by Gabriel Teixidó: Boxster, Hamilton and Lluna (from top to bottom).

2. From the FOSCARINI catalog, the models: Manta (top) and Folio (bottom), two designs from Pio and Tito Toso.

3. MARSET produce the model Atlas X3, designed by Joan Gaspar.

4. From the brand IGUZZINI, a creation by Pamio, the Vision PL 270.

5. Tubular 4S from the brand DELTALIGHT.

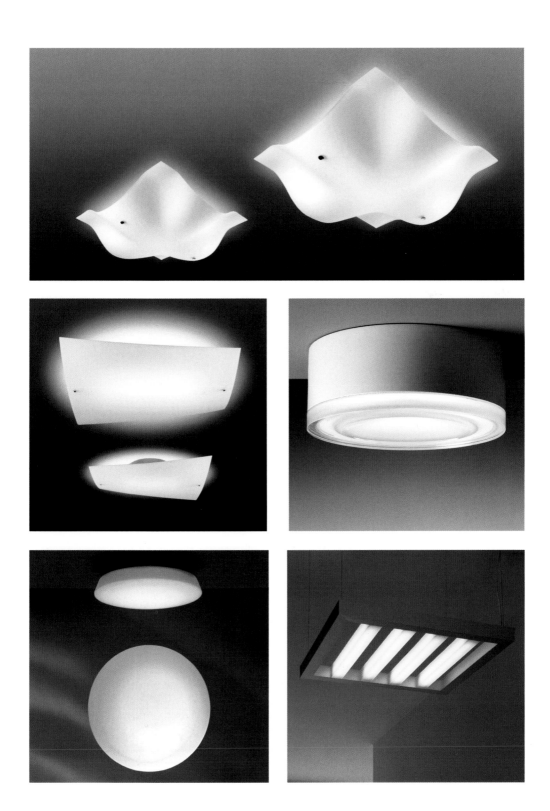

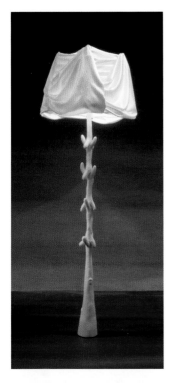

standard lamp

Standard lamps are used as much to provide overall illumination as for areas in which particular activities such as reading or sewing are carried out. Although there are those which project light into the space thanks to a parabolic dish, most of them tend to stand out in the area in which they are situated due to their marked verticality. The light they give is generally quite strong to enable tasks to be carried out effectively. They were traditionally inseparable companions of armchairs, but they have gradually become more and more independent and have started occupying strategic places in rooms and passages. In order to acquire a certain degree of intimacy, those with regulable intensity often become the main source of light in a particular area.

Their use is also extended to that of decoration and some are as much a functional as a decorative element. This is the case of the avant-garde Asana (KUNDALINI) or the Lamp Palo from ELITE with a structure in iron and coconut that looks like a skyscraper. Some pieces, such as the model Akis from CLASSICON or Wave and Ice from DERIN, are very sculptural. On the other side of the coin, we find the most minimalist designs such as Tulipe de LIGNE ROSET, a piece of illumination in its the minimal expression. We find forms based on organic elements, this is the case of Morning Glory Flame (AQUA CREATIONS), and those that remind us of imaginary space: in the form of a UFO, the model Tornasol de SANTA & COLE. And, of course, there is also room for art as is shown by a number of lamps by Dalí which are commercialized by BD.

1. From ELITE, two models from the Nito collection (left) and from the Panama collection (right).

2. ARTEMIDE produce Yin, a design by Carlotta de Bevilacqua.

3. The firm SAWAYA & MORONI present Sasha (left) and Ingrid (right), designed by O.M. Ungers.

AFRA AND TOBIA SCARPA

Afra Bianchin (1937) and Tobia Scarpa (1935) have formed a team that has been a point of reference for the entire design world since 1958 when they started working in the glass sector for Venini in Murano. From among the pieces of furniture designed exclusively for Cassina, the armchair Soriano, which won the Golden Compass Award in 1970 and the armchair 925, which forms part of the permanent exhibition of the Museum of Modern Art in New York, stand out. They have also formed part of the Castiglioni team and designed for Flos. Of the pieces that they have produced for B&B Italia, Coronado and Erasmo are the best known. In addition to having also designed for Maxalto and Molteni, they have taken on responsibilities for the image campaigns of Benetton in Europe and America.

Profile

>>

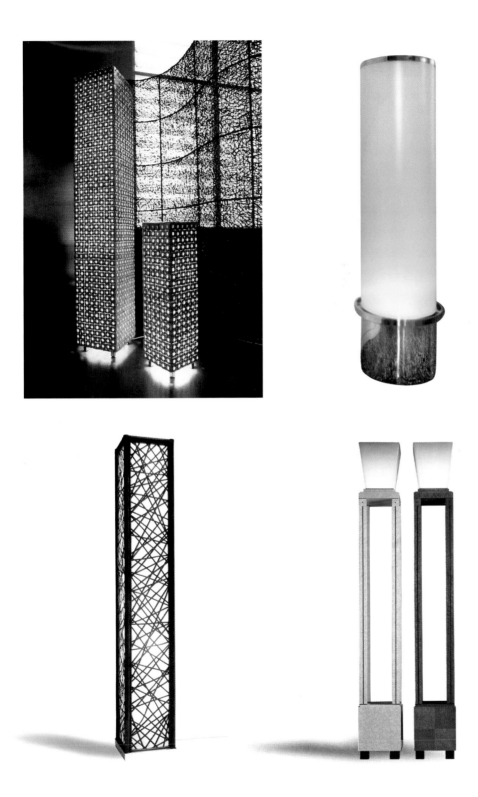

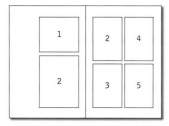

1. CATTELAN ITALIA commercialize Channel de Menguzzato & Nascimben.

2. Two products from QUASAR: Maxara (bottom) and High & Mighty (top).

3. Große Lampe from Johanna Hitzler.

4. A model from the FONTANA ARTE catalog, Hashira.

5. From QUASAR, a design by Paul Imbrechts: Muranissimo.

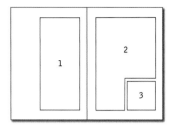

1. Model Dolcetta from VANLUX, proposed by B.LUX.

2. From KUNDALINI, standard lamps (from left to right): Shakti by Marzio Rusconi Clerici, Ray Lumi by Gregorio Spini (top) and Sama by Gregorio Spini (bottom).

3. FONTANA ARTE produce this design by Marc Krusin: Lantern.

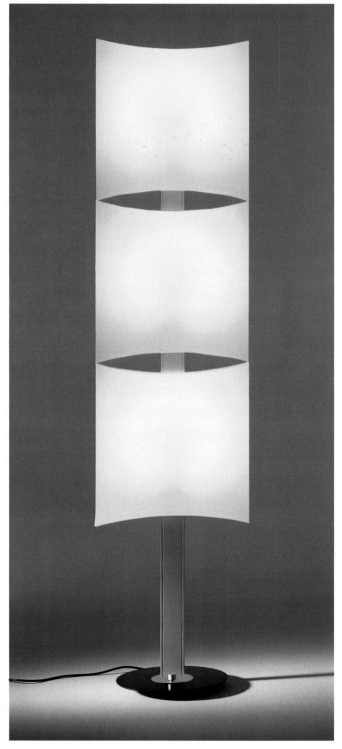

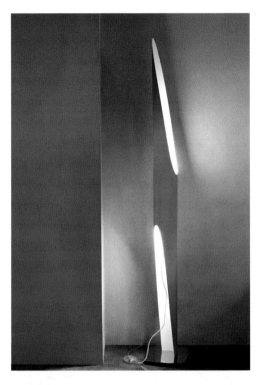

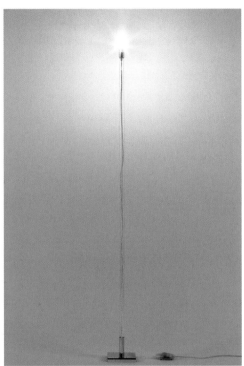

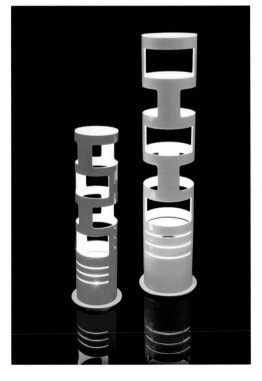

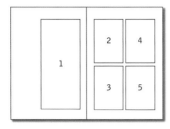

1. Luisa Calvi, Mauro Merlini and Carlos Moya have designed Stix for Candle (FONTANA ARTE).

2. ROLF BENZ produce the lamp Palo by Joachim Nees.

3. From the brand GREEN, a design by Christian Gori.

4. A product from PALLUCO, Acquarius by Filippo Dell'Orto.

5. Bamboo is a lamp from VIABIZZUNO.

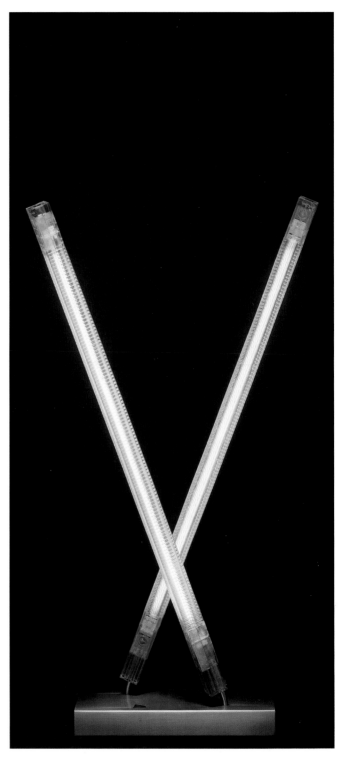

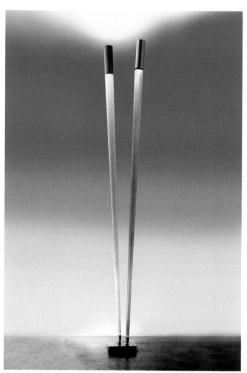

Only lights 97 STANDARD LAMPS

1. Valzer is a model from PALLU-CO, created by Pamio Design.
2. Two designs by Christian Gori for GREEN.
3. Gigantic in two different versions from the brand VIBIA.

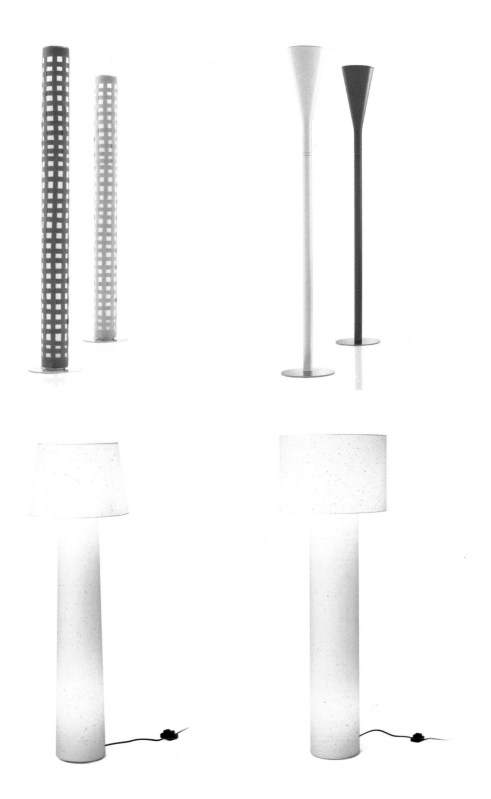

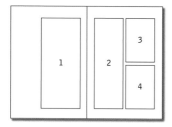

1. Model Ondalina from MARSET.

2. Aziz Sariyer designed these lamps: Ice (top) and Wave (bottom) from the brand DERIN.

3. A product from VIBIA: Stemp.

4. SAWAYA & MORONI present Sora by John Maeda. An interactive standard lamp with acoustic sensor which varies the color and form of the light.

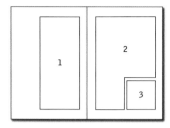

1. Muranissimo is another product
   from QUASAR designed by Paul
   Imbrechts.

2. KUNDALINI produce Ojas (top)
   and Sama (bottom) created by
   Gregorio Spini.

3. Giotto TR is from the MURANODUE
   catalog. A proposal by FIRME
   DI VETRO.

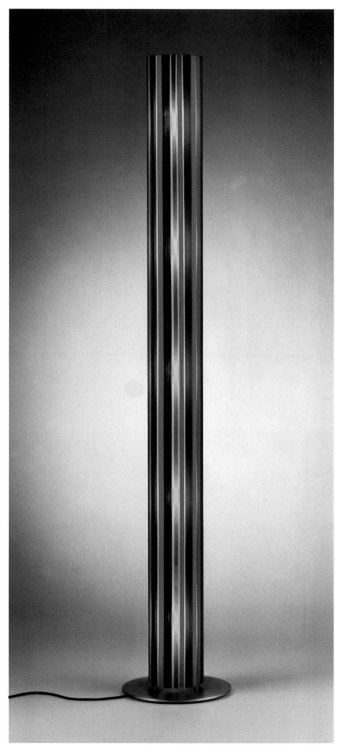

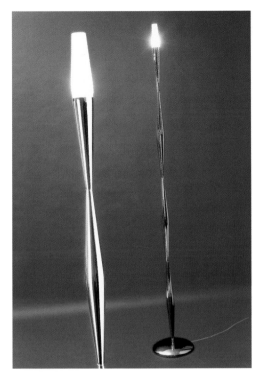

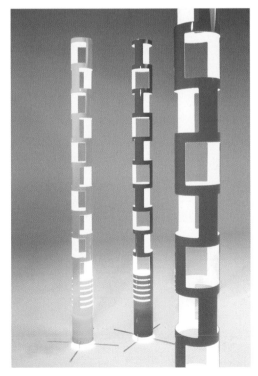

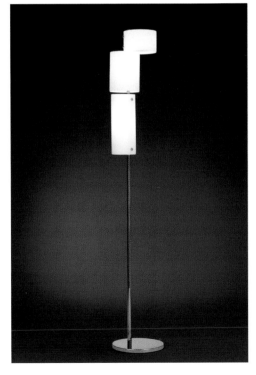

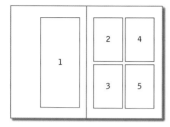

1. FOTOSATR propose this design by Ana Ruiz de la Prada: Jazzambi.

2. From BELUX, the model Twilight.

3. The CARPYEN catalog includes this creation by Gabriel Teixidó, Aurita.

4. A standard lamp from PENTA.

5. Havana is a product from the brand FOSCARINI from the hands of Jozeph Forakis.

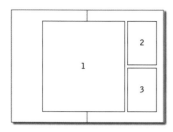

1. FOSCARINI produce these standard lamps. On this page, a design by Marc Sadler, Mite, for which he was awarded the "Compasso d'Oro" in 2001. On the following page, top, Totem, created by Valerio Bottin. Each one of its three elements lights up independently. Bottom, a model from Luca Nichetto and Gianpietro Gai : Thor.

2. The brand ARTEMIDE present this standard lamp from Jan Van-Lierde: Multiper.

3. A model from DAB for the exterior, Pass.

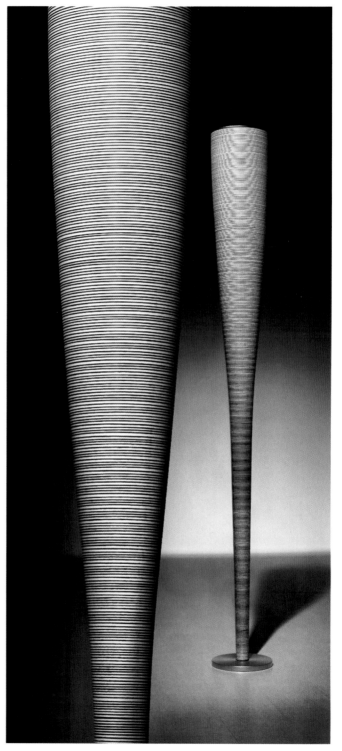

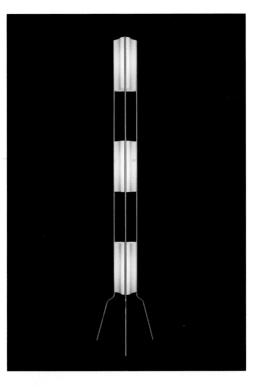

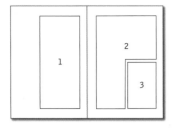

1. Burney Koelemij designed Emily for QUASAR.

2. Luume is a design from Massimo Belloni for PENTA. To the right, Kimilla from the same brand and creator.

3. Marco Zanuso Jr. is the creator of Minimal, a product from FONTANA ARTE.

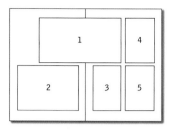

1. KUNDALINI present this design by Gregorio Spini: Lila.

2. Two products from the PALLU-CO catalog. Dot (right) contains a mechanism that allows the light to be regulated with no more than a movement.

3. Model Column from VIBIA.

4. Rigel is a design from Carlotta de Bevilacqua produced by ARTEMIDE, which emits chromatic light from its front part and indirect halogen light from its upper part.

5. From the brand QUASAR, the model Helicon.

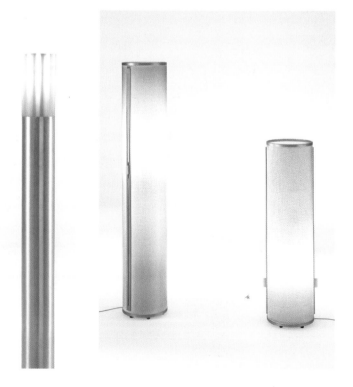

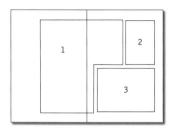

1. From ILLU STRATION, a creation from Alexander Pernitschka and Mary-Ann Williams: Xolo-Flokati Filz.

2. Aqua Regia is a creation from Ayala Serfaty and is included in the catalog Light Of My Life from AQUA CREATIONS.

3. The model Abat-jour from PA-LLUCO is a standard lamp that gives off indirect and diffused light. Metal base varnished with epoxidic dust with titanium finish.

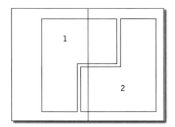

1. Model One by One from BELUX.

2. These models belong to the AQUA CREATIONS catalog and were designed by Ayala Serfaty. Top, Horn. Bottom, to the left, Morning Glory Flame, and, to the right, Maestro.

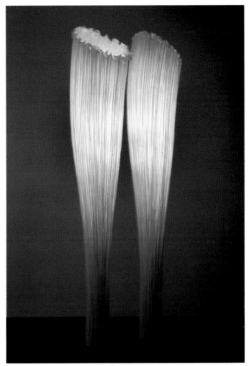

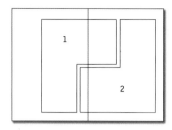

1. A proposal from FIRME DI VE-
   TRO, different versions of the mo-
   del Giukó, from the catalog from
   ITRE.

2. Model Papyrus (top) and two
   lamps designed by Henk Elenga
   in different finishes (bottom)
   from QUASAR.

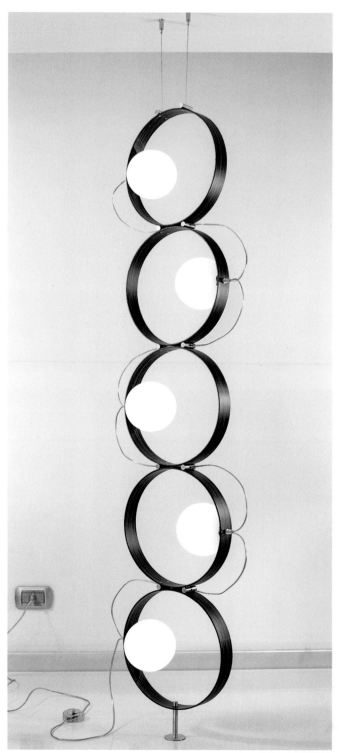

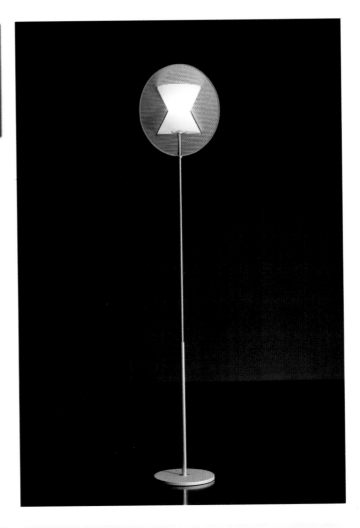

1. Massimo Scolari created Lampi for GIORGETTI.

2. Libra belongs to the META-LARTE catalog.

3. BD holds the exclusive for the commercialization of these designs by Salvador Dalí. From Left to right: Cajones, Muletas and Bracelli.

>>

MATTEO THUN

Matteo Thun was born in 1952 in Bozen (South Tirol) and studied under the supervision of Oskar Kokoshka at the Salzburg Academia. He graduated in Architecture at the University of Florence in 1976 and some years later, in 1980, he founded the Memphis Design Group along with Ettore Sottsass. From 1983 to 1996, he taught at the University of Applied Arts of Vienna while also working in his own studio which he established in 1984 and which, today, has developed into a team of 50 architects, designers and graphic designers that undertake projects around the world. Matteo Thun has always tried, in all of the areas in which he has developed his professional activity, to find more than a language in which to expound himself. His objective is to obtain "echo and non-ego", which is to say transcendence rather than personal satisfaction.

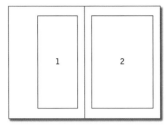

1. Rodolfo Dordoni created Lumiere (top) and Defne Koz designed Dress (bottom) for FOSCARINI.

2. The studio PearsonLloyd designed the following models for CLASSICON: Aleos (top) and Dione (bottom).

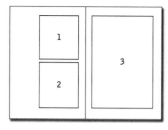

1. One of the three versions of the lamp from INGO MAURER Little Big Lamp.

2. Castore is a standard lamp from the ARTEMIDE catalog.

3. Varios models from the firm HK.

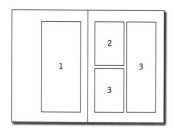

1. A design by Lluís Porqueras and Cristian Díez from one of the SANTA & COLE catalogs. This series proposes the incorporation of a simple magnate in order to bring up to date a classical form and to give it a new meaning. The height of the screen can be adjusted by means of the friction between the two metal tubes that make up the stem which are united by a double magnate inserted into a plastic support.

2. VINÇON includes this model from the brand MARSET in their catalog.

3. Swing (Top), Gondola and Tiptoe (Left and right respectively, bottom) are three models from VIBIA.

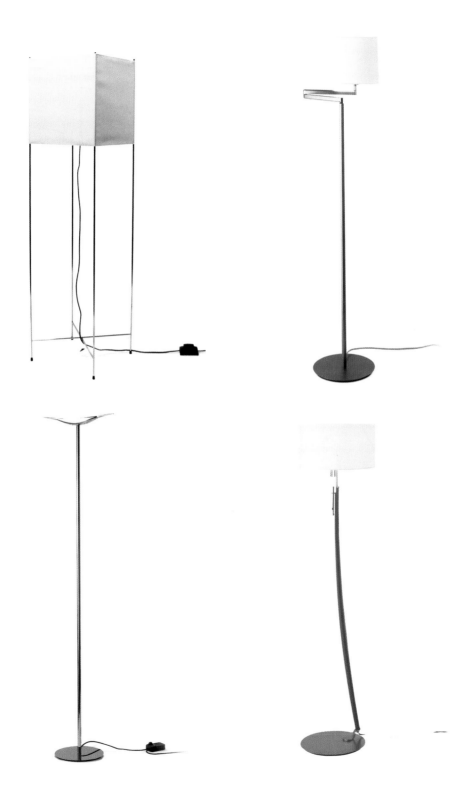

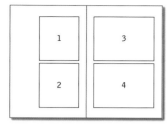

| 1 | 3 |
| 2 | 4 |

1. Photograph courtesy of SANTA & COLE. The standard lamp Tornasol is a design from Alfredo Arribas.

2. Cónica is a product from CARPYEN.

3. Balance is a model from VIBIA.

4. Lievore Altherr Molina's stidio designed the model Pia for METALARTE.

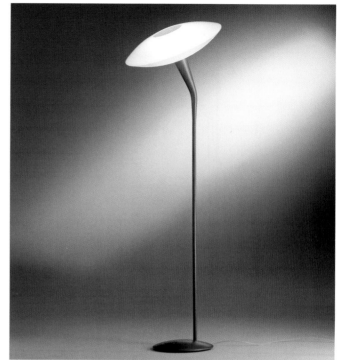

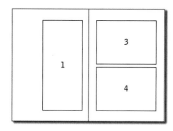

1. DE PADOVA present this creation from Phil Luithlen: the DT Light.

2. Efqus is a product from QUASAR.

3. PALLUCO present this design by Mariano Fortuny and Madrazo, Fortuny (1907).

4. Three standard lamps produced by ARTEK.

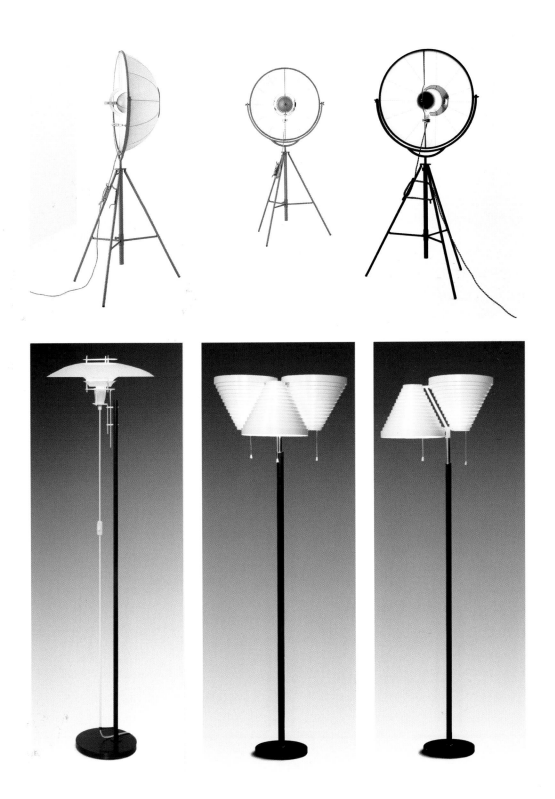

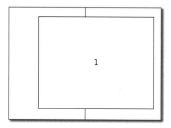

1. The model Akis, from Mauro Bertoldini, in the center of the image alongside other lamps from CLASSICON.

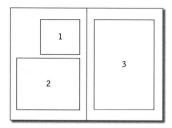

1. ARTEMIDE propose this lamp, created by Michele De Lucchi and Gerhard Reichert.

2. Pelota is a standard lamp model from the hands of Daniela Puppa and commercialized by FONTANA ARTE

3. ANTHOLOGIE QUARTET commercialize Polycolor by Patrick Knoch.

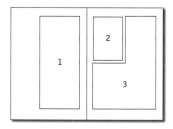

1. OLIGO produce this design by Markus Heckhaussen and Ralf Keferstein: Ampelmann.

2. El model Turn On from AAN-UIT in red.

3. GREEN present these three lamps designed by Christian Gori.

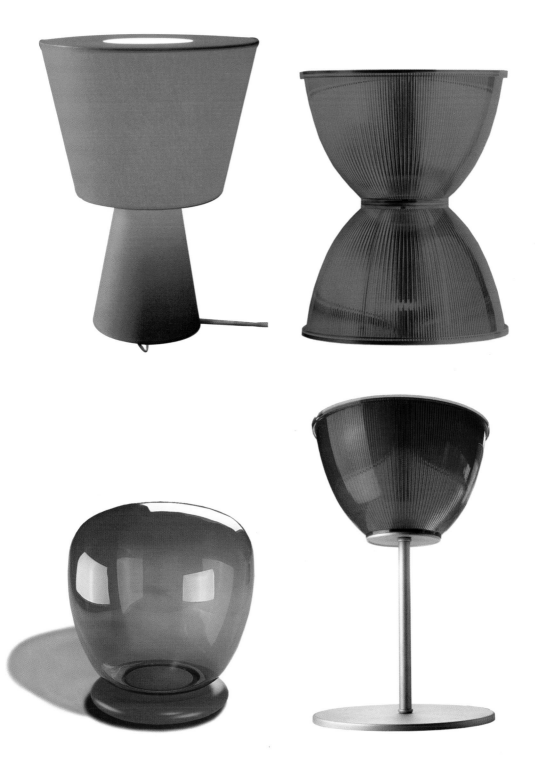

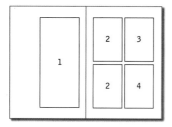

1. FOSCARINI produce Orbital by Ferruccio Laviani.

2. Tulip is a model by Sybille Mevissen from the brand QUASAR.

3. Jan des Bouvrie designed Rollight for QUASAR.

4. Marilyn is a product from the brand MURANODUE of the group FIRME DI VETRO. It is a creation from Carlo Nason.

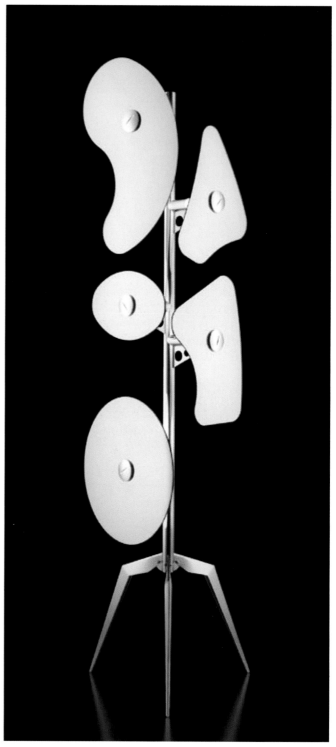

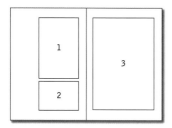

1. ILUMINACIÓN PETER JAHN distribute this model from the brand BERND BEISSE.

2. This lamp with a handle, Yang Touch, belongs to the catalog from ARTEMIDE.

3. QUASAR produce these designs from Jos Muller: Miru and Omega (the two bottom images on the left).

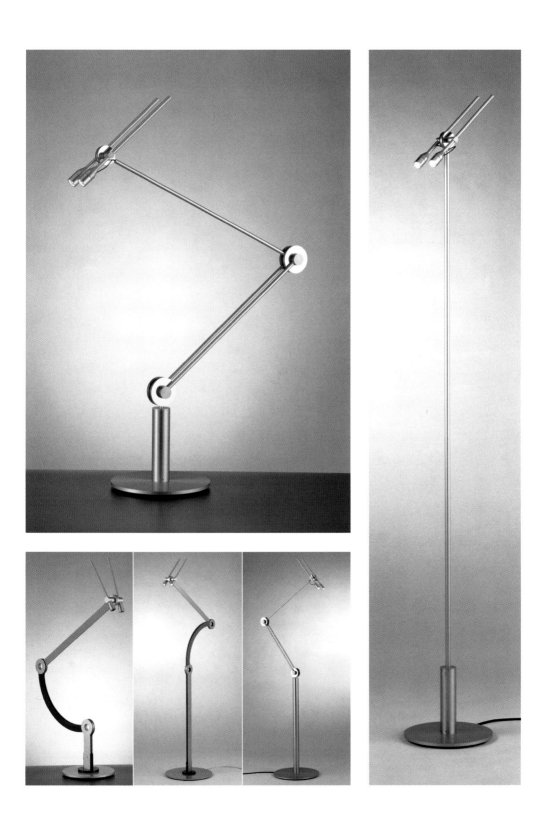

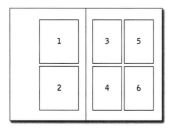

1. An accessory from the brand CONMOTO for candles.

2. Spazio is a model from the firm PALLUCO created by Carlo Tamborini.

3. Sextans is a model from ARTEMIDE from the hands of Italo Rota and Alessandro Pedretti.

4. Daniela Puppa designed Charms for FONTANA ARTE.

5. Another proposal from SLD produced by ZLAMP, the Bezz Pie.

6. Little Big Lamp is a creation from INGO MAURER.

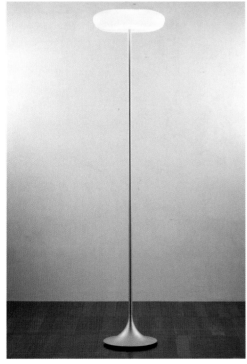

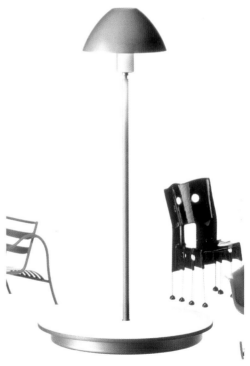

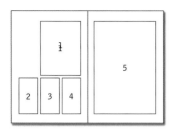

1. Ray Bow, designed by Gregorio Spini, is a producto from KUN-DALINI.

2. B.LUX propose this model Adorable from D. Fortunado (VANLUX).

3. Lamp Bolla from Harry & Camila, produced by FONTANA ARTE.

4. PENTA commercialize this model, China, by Nicola Gallizia.

5. Inout by Ramón Úbeda and Otto Canalda is a lamp produced by METALARTE from the Metalab collection.

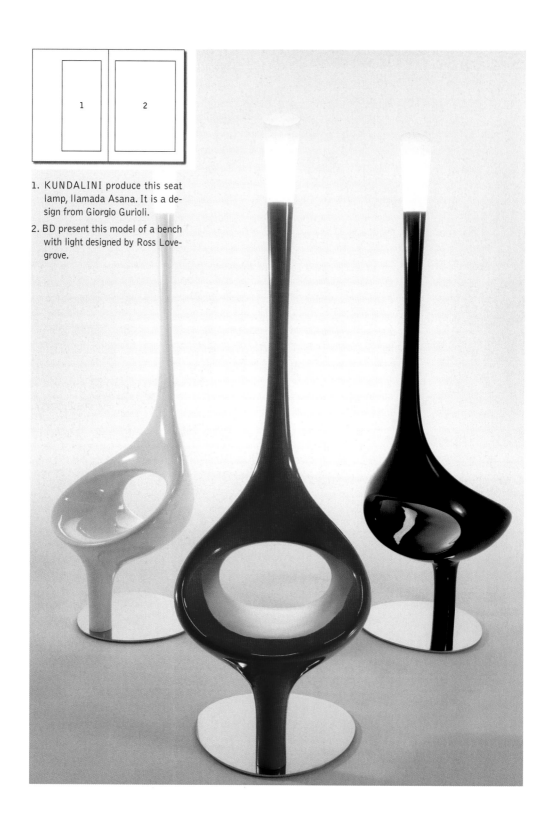

1. KUNDALINI produce this seat lamp, llamada Asana. It is a design from Giorgio Gurioli.

2. BD present this model of a bench with light designed by Ross Lovegrove.

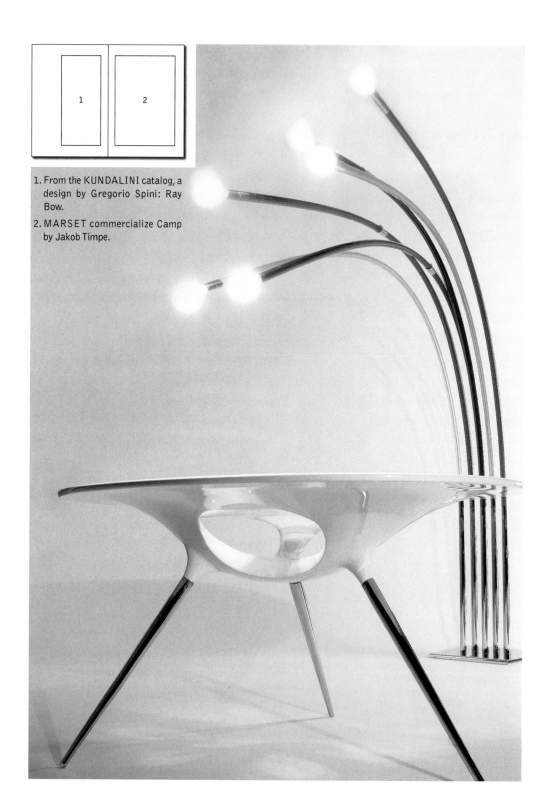

| 1 | 2 |

1. From the KUNDALINI catalog, a design by Gregorio Spini: Ray Bow.

2. MARSET commercialize Camp by Jakob Timpe.

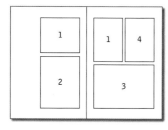

1. H2Ot (on this page) and H3Ot (on the following) are two products from the brand VIABIZ-ZUNO.

2. Anello from DIEMO ALFONS.

3. Prototype is a design from Bernhard Dessecker and Ingo Maurer which is included in the INGO MAURER catalog.

4. From IGUZZINI, this design by Massimo and Leila Vignelli and David Law: Downtown 2.

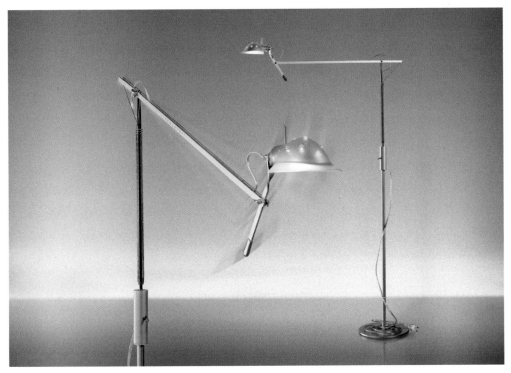

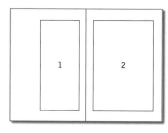

1. Hydra is a product from ESSEN-
   TIA.
2. MOBLES 114 BARCELONA is
   the official distributor in Spain
   for Akari Light Sculpture.

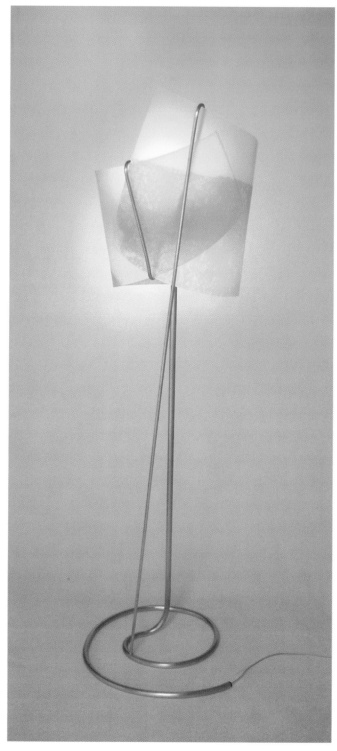

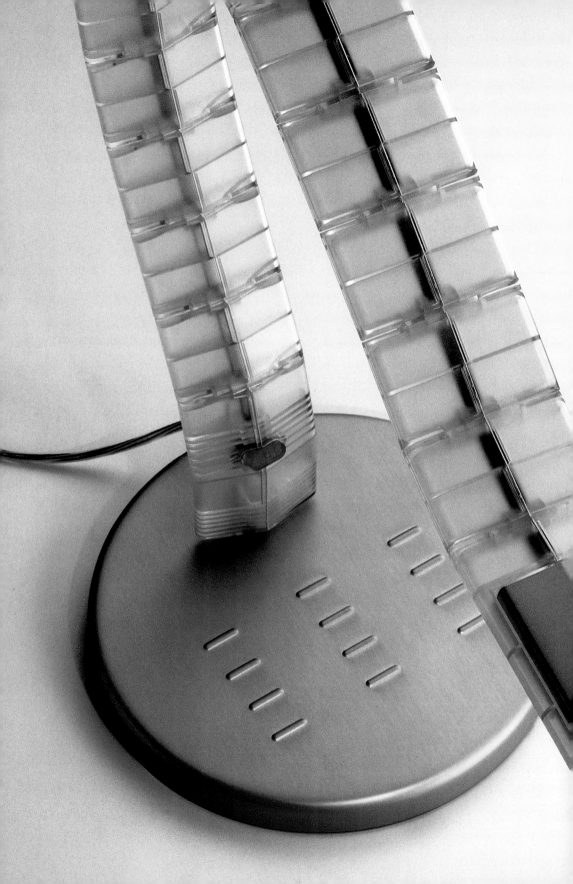

table lamps

From ancient times, human beings have desired to continue their tasks after sunset. The Mesopotamians wished to defy the laws of nature and continue reading after nightfall. The Romans also wanted to carry on studying their documents after supper. They had to find a light to illuminate their investigation. It has been the electric light, however, that has led to the real revolution when it comes to combating darkness and allowing work or leisure activities to extend to the 24 hours of a day. Table lamps are the most faithful ally of human activity. Our enjoyment of greater concentration and efficiency depends on their design and quality.

The list of pieces of illumination of this type is long and it ranges from the most functional to the most decorative: those of adjustable height, flexible ones that can be inclined according to necessities, a hybrid of these that has a rigid component and another that can be bent so as to obtain a greater area of illumination, those based on the idea of constant tension, those that move to and fro on their base, those with various arms and light sources, those that reflect off a mirror, the traditional library ones, the fluorescent ones, The LEDs, the classical ones with a glass or ceramic base, those that are no more than a beautified light bulb as well as the more artistic ones. Designers such as those from the studios PearsonLloyd, Philippe Starck, Ferruccio Laviani, or Antoni Citterio, among others, develop their own particular interpretation of the table or work lamp in this section.

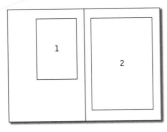

1. Marianelli Design by Barbara Sordina designed Nina for PEN-TA.

2. From the group FIRME DI VETRO, the models Ghost (top), Atmosfera and Cino (bottom, left and right respectively) produced by MURANODUE.

RODOLFO DORDONI

Rodolfo Dordoni was born in Milan in 1954. He graduated in architecture at the Polytechnic University of Milan in 1979. After various experiences in different architectural studios, he started working in the area of industrial design. He worked on strategies of image ranging from those for products to those of the communication sectors. From 1979 to 1989, he took on the responsibilities of the artistic direction and coordinated the image for Cappellini. He has practiced as a consultant and designer for different companies apart from his activity as architect and designer of commercial establishments, stands and pavilions. Rodolfo Dordoni has collaborated with Acerbis, Arteluce, Artemide, Moroso, Tisenttanta, Driade, Venini, Flos, Fontana Arte, Lema, Fiam, Foscarini, Minotti, Dolce & Gabbana, Molteni, De Sede, Halifax, and Flou among others.

Profile

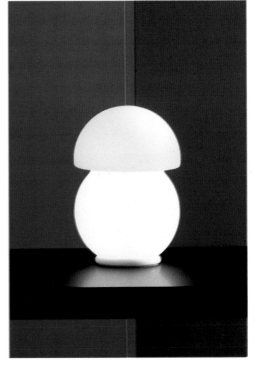

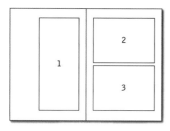

1. Other proposals from ALT LU-
   CIALTERNATIVE, the model Ais
   (top) and Ais T Rosa FC (Bottom).

2. Also from the group FIRM E DI
   VETRO, Bacco 1, 2, 3 (left) from
   ITRE and RX CO (right) a brand
   belonging to MURANODUE.

3. Gregorio Spini designed this table
   lamp, Sama, for KUNDALINI.

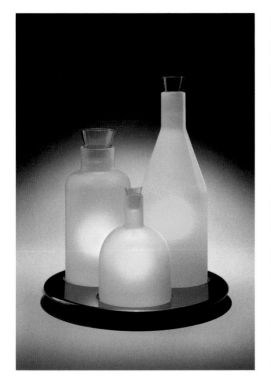

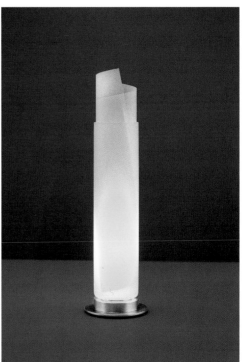

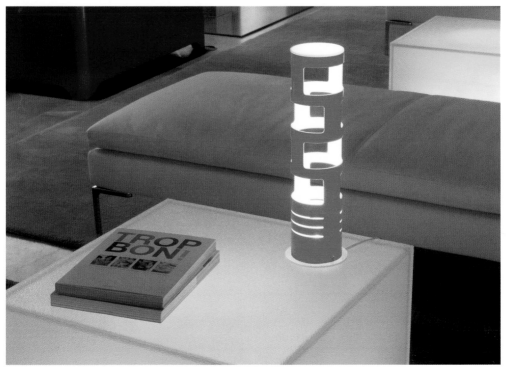

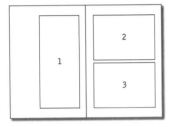

1. Plodule is a design from Karim Rashid for ARTEMIDE.
2. FOSCARINI present Dress from Defne Koz.
3. INDUSTRIA191 propose the model QTL.

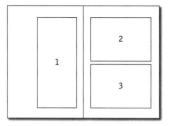

1. METALARTE produce this design by Richard Ferrer: Zoom.

2. Jordi Llopis designed Concentra for METALARTE.

3. Lamp Domo by Antoni Arola and Jordi Tamayo is a product from the brand METALARTE.

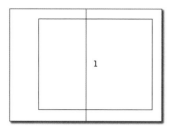

1. Next to these lines, Shape Yellow,
   On the following page, top, Candle
   Design Blue (left) and Tube Yel-
   low-Green (right). Bottom,
   Chiller (left) and Candle Classic
   Top Yellow (right). All are mod-
   els from TRAXON.

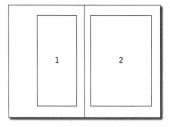

1. ALBUM produce this design by Tanzi Design, the model Tonic.

2. Top, Ambience White Kinka (left) and Rotondo Blue Kinka (right). Bottom, the model Polaris Red. All are products from TRAXON.

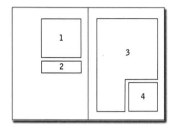

1. Tactic is another proposal from the firm ALBUM.

2. VINÇON propose these models: Light Volumes from VILA IMPORT (left) and Hectárea from MARSET ILUMINACIÓN.

3. Top, Nipotino (left) and Zia (Right). Bottom, Zia, Zio and Nipotino, all are products from LUCEPLAN.

4. DAB propose Empty.

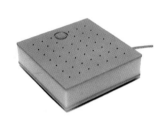

PEARSONLLOYD

Tom Lloyd and Luke Pearson associated themselves in 1997 and founded PearsonLloyd, a multidisciplined design consultancy located in a studio in Whitechapel in East London. Their activities range from product design or strategic investigation to architecture.

Luke Pearson was trained as an industrial designer and later completed his studies with a master in furniture design at the Royal College of Art. Prior to his experience in PearsonLloyd, he worked along side Ross Lovegrove in Studio X in London. Tom Lloyd studied furniture and industrial design. Before associating with Pearson, he formed part of Pentagrama with Daniel Weil. They both teach in the Ecole Cantonale d'art de Laussane in Switzerland.

Profile

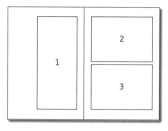

1. Two aspects of Maria, a table lamp from VIABIZZUNO.

2. Patricia Urquiola and Eliana Gerotto designed Bague for FOSCARINI.

3. A proposal from B.LUX from the brand VANLUX, designed by Quim Larrea and Gonzalo Milá: San Marco.

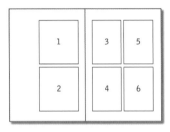

1. Cocò is a model from FOSCARI-NI, designed by Aldo Cibic.

2. Karim Rashid designed Blob for FOSCARINI.

3. ARTEMIDE commercialize Sorry Mama by Ernesto Gismon-di.

4. Another creation by Karim Ras-hid, this time for the brand ARTE-MIDE: Time & Space.

5. FOSCARINI, produced by Lenin, from Ferruccio Laviani.

6. Bellatrix, by Carlotta de Bevilac-qua belongs to the ARTEMIDE catalog. It is not only a lamp, but an air purifier as well.

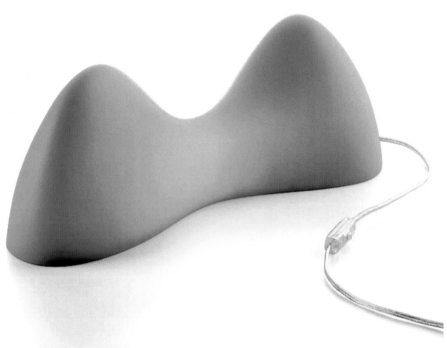

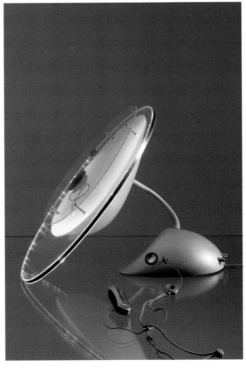

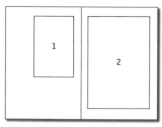

1. A design by Marc Sadler for FOSCARINI: Lite.

2. From the brand FOSCARINI, Elfo, by Denis Santachiara.

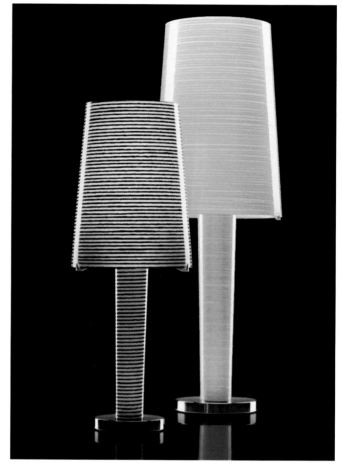

ALBERTO LIEVORE

This designer and architect from the Argentine has produced a large number of works of great quality and coherence which have been recognized in Spain with the award of the National Design prize (1999). In 1977, he settled in Barcelona and set up the Grupo Berenguer along with Jorge Pensi, Norberto Chaves and Oriol Pibernat. This team understood design as an activity that not only involved the conception of a product, but the development of its graphic image and its promotion as well. The furniture designed for Perobell or Kron with serene lines are from this period. Later, he started to work independently and in 1991, Jeannette Alter and Manel Molina joined his studio and extended the studio's activities to product design, interior design, architectural projects, teaching, packaging, consulting and art direction for various companies such as Andreu World o Santa & Cole.

Profile

>>

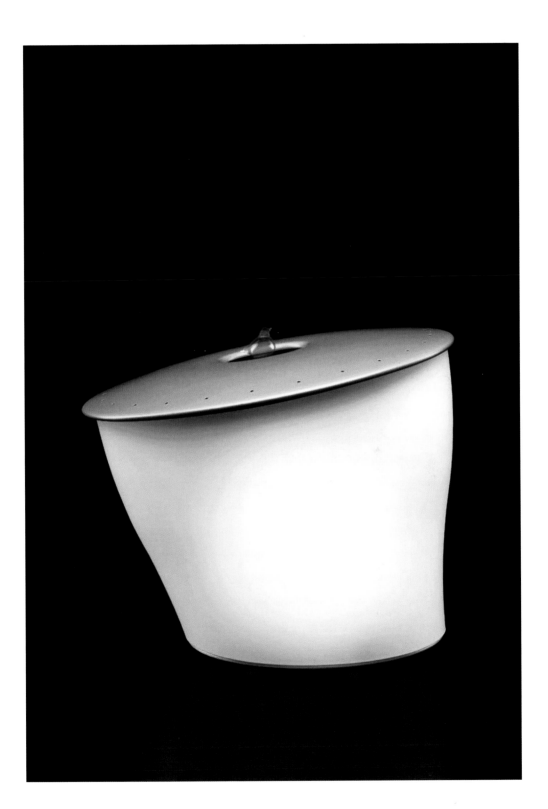

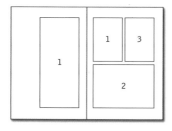

1. New interpretation of the K6 lamp of 1985, inspired in the pictorial world of Wassily Kandinsky. It is one of the novelties from FOSCARINI designed by Adam D. Tihany and Joseph Mancini. In the images on this page, in different versions, and, on the following, a detail.

2. Gregorio Spini designed Tat for KUNDALINI.

3. FOSCARINI commercialize Lampoon by Aldo Cibic.

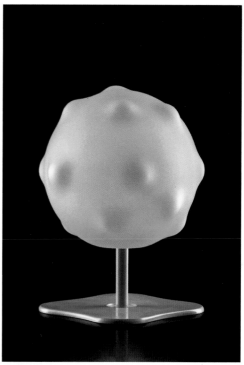

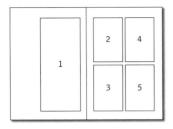

1. Bulb is a design from INGO MAURER.

2. A table lamp from the INGO MAURER catalog, Bellissima Brutta.

3. Litelight is a lamp from AQUA CREATIONS.

4. ILLU STRATION propose this creation from Alexander Pernitschka and Mary-Ann Williams: Globe.

5. Karim Rashid designed the model Blob MXL for the brand FOSCARINI.

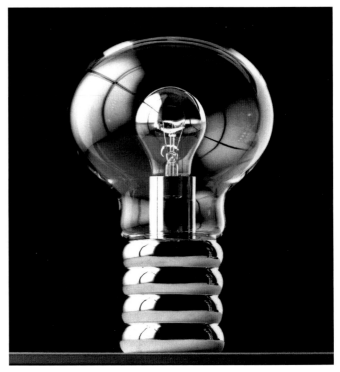

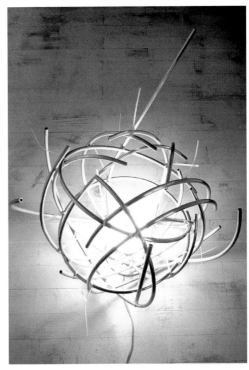

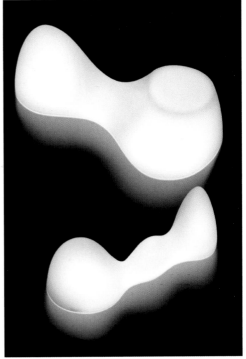

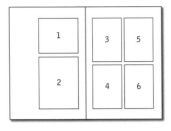

1. Accento is a very versatile product from the brand ALBUM.

2. A design by Bernhard Dessecker, which we can see in the INGO MAURER catalog: Topolino.

3. Yoyo is an amusing proposal from FLOTOTTO.

4. Rainy Day is a creation from Kazuhiro Yamanaka commercialized by PALLUCCO.

5. VINÇON present this model from the brand PROPAGANDIST, the table lamp Mr P.

6. Lumibär is a product from the ELMAR FLÖTOTTO catalog.

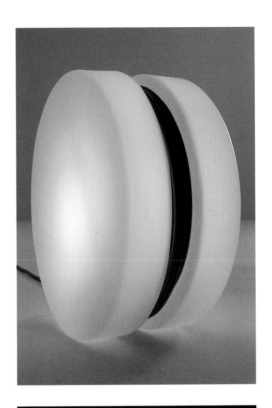

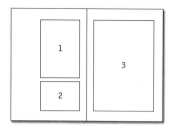

1. Led Bench is a proposal from INGO MAURER.

2. Verform is a proposal from L.I.N.

3. ELMAR FLÖTOTTO include these models in their catalog: Eggo (top and bottom, on the left) and Pinguin (right).

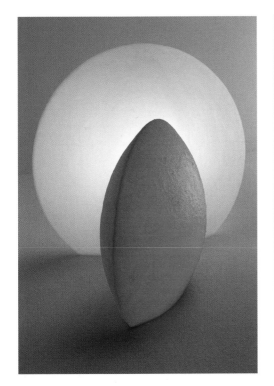
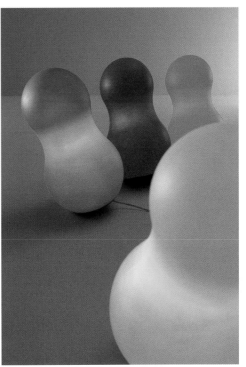

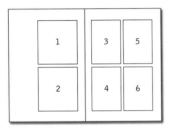

1. From the group FIRME DI VE-
   TRO, the model Finn Light CO,
   from the brand MURANODUE.

2. Take is a design from Ferruccio
   Laviani for KARTELL.

3. From the collection New Classic
   by PENTA, the model Pascià.

4. B.LUX - VANLUX propose this
   design by J.Novell and J.Puig, the
   lamp Jackie.

5. ILLU STRATION present Snake
   de Alexander Pernitschka and
   Mary-Ann Williams.

6. Model Ed, commercialized by
   ELMAR FLÖTOTTO, in different
   colors.

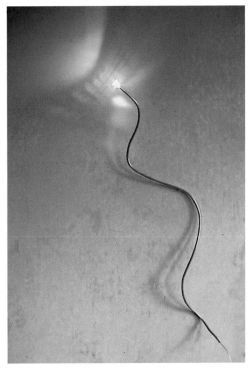

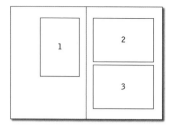

1. FONTANA ARTE commercialize this design by Daniela Puppa: Charms.

2. From FONTANA ARTE, Amélie, a design by Harry & Camila.

3. LOOKILUZ propose the model Sixtie.

PIERO LISSONI

Piero Lissoni was born in 1956. Having finalized his studies in Architecture at the University of Milan, he started to work for Molteni and Lema. In 1986, he established the Lissoni studio in Milan along with Nicoletta Canesi where he developed projects in architecture, interior design, graphic design, industrial design and art direction and corporate image for some of the most outstanding companies of the sector. Some of the companies with which Lissoni has collaborated are Porro, Living, Matteograssi, Bofia Cucine, Artemide, Foscarini, Kartell, Driade, Cassina or the Benetton Group. Piero Lissoni is one of the most outstanding figures in the world of Italian design inspired by minimalism. However, he would reject this label in an attempt to escape from the limitations that it would imply and prefers to talk about simplicity. Concepts such as the honesty and purity of form are also essential to his creations.

Profile

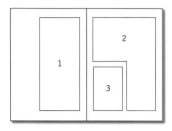

1. Rodolfo Dordoni designed Bijou (top) and Lumiere (bottom) for FOSCARINI.

2. Three products from the brand PENTA: top, C'hi by Massimo Belloni (left), China by Nicola Gallizia (right) and, bottom, Luume also by Massimo Belloni.

3. Marzio Rusconi Clerici created Padma for KUNDALINI.

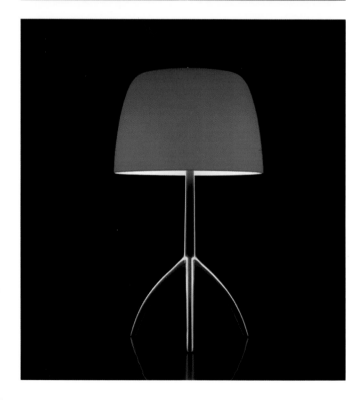

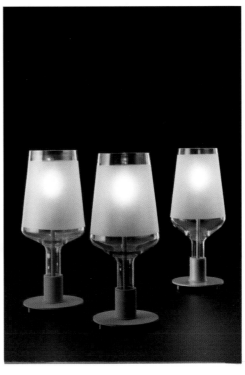

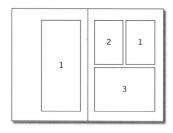

1. PENTA produce different versions of the model Kimilla by Massimo Belloni (next to these lines). On the following page, the table lamp, China.

2. FOSCARINI commercialize this design by Lievore Asociados: Esa.

3. From ARTEMIDE, this table model, Logico, by Michele De Lucchi and Gerhard Reichert.

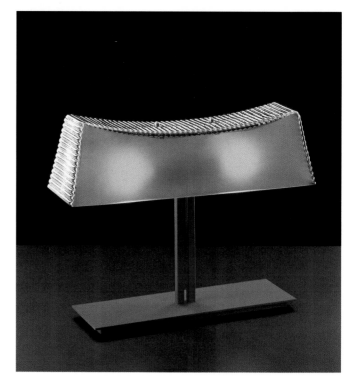

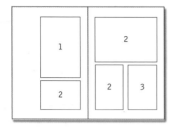

1. Moncoeur (top) and Laperlel (bottom) are two models from NICO HEILMANN.

2. Different versions of the lamp Escargot from NICO HEILMANN.

3. Another version of Laperlel from NICO HEILMANN.

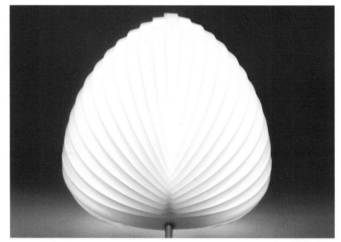

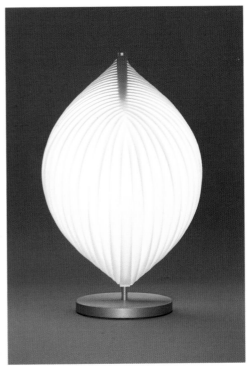

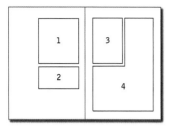

1. Two table lamps, included in the INGO MAURER catalog, created by Nils Jann, the B96 N°1 and the B96 N°2.

2. VICTORIA propose the model Magic Box.

3. Japan is a lamp designed by Gabriel Teixidó for the firm CARPYEN.

4. Two versions of Bodona, a model from the brand PENTA, created by Massimo Belloni.

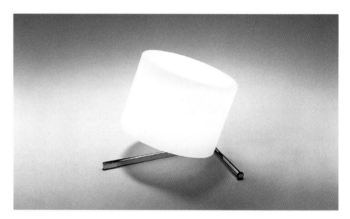

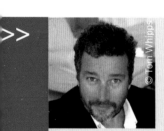

PHILIPPE STARCK

There are many who consider Philippe Starck to be the great Guru of contemporary design. He has worked in more or less every area of design from interiors such as The Royalton and The Paramount in New York, which he converted into two new classics of the hotel world, to motorcycles and even kitchen utensils. In the 1980's, he started designing furniture for the most representative companies in the sector. His models stand out for the way in which they reinterpret the aesthetics of a bygone age in new materials. Philippe Starck is an arduous defender of the environment and the human being. He is one who believes that design can change the world and aspires to "create greater happiness with fewer things". He has received numerous prizes and his creations can be found in museums all around the world.

Profile

© Toni Whipps

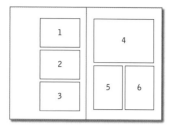

1. From the brand MOX, a model created by Christian Deuber and Jörg Boner: Bond.
2. A proposal from the company WK WOHNEN.
3. B.LUX - VANLUX present Julia and Julieta by M. Ybarguengoitia.
4. ARTEMIDE produce these models. Castore, a design by Michele De Lucchi and Huub Ubbens.
5. FIRME DI VETRO propose this model produced by MURANO-DUE, Paralume.
6. DAB present this design by David Abad: Ilde T2.

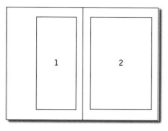

1. Two products from PENTA: C'hi
   from Massimo Belloni (top) and
   Kori from Otto Moon (bottom).

2. Top, Luzia (left) and Luzilla
   (right). Bottom, two versions of
   Medusina. All from the ALBUM
   catalog.

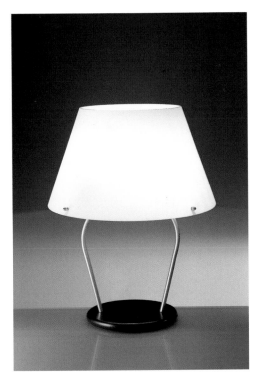

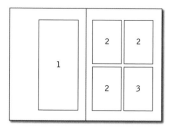

1. From the collection New Classic from PENTA, two designs by Gaia Bellavia, the model Bon Ton (top) and Desir (bottom).

2. FITZ LICHT produce the following models: top, Boveda (left) and Globo (right). Bottom, Bologna.

3. Marco Zanuso created this model from the brand MARSET: Montana.

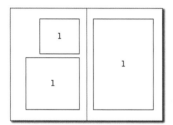

1. Different products from the brand FONTANA ARTE: Chiara (top), Urka, by Alessandro Piva (bottom), and Sospiro in different colores (on the following page).

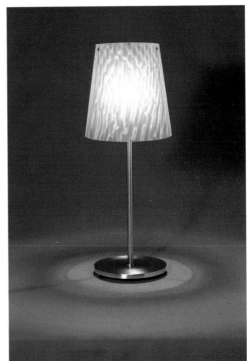

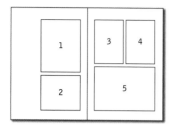

1. VIABIZZUNO produce the model Fil.

2. A design by Adam D. Tihany for ROSSI DI ALBIZZATE, a multi-functional piece called Nesting.

3. From ANTHOLOGIE QUARTET, a design by Robert Wettstein, the lamp Schwan.

4. AAN-UIT produce this creation by Marc Th. Van der Voorn: Turn On.

5. Struppler is a table lamp from the INGO MAURER catalog.

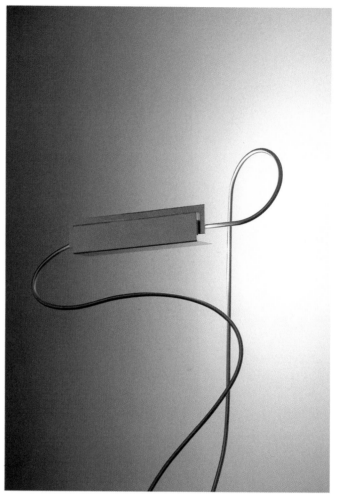

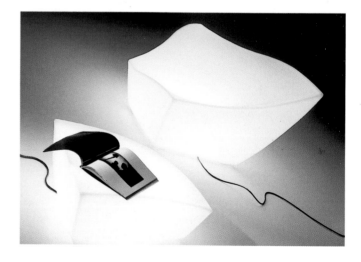

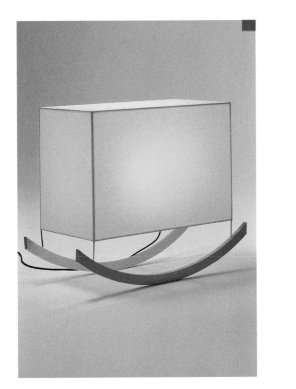

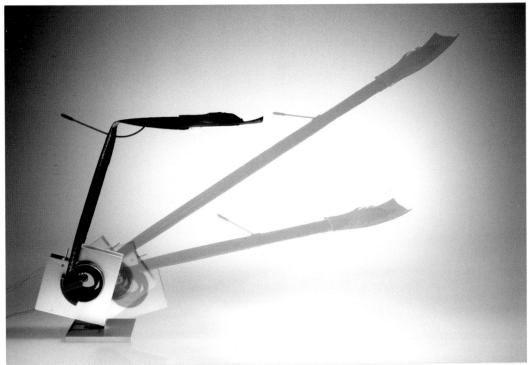

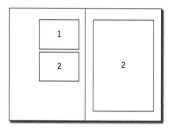

1. VIABIZZUNO produce the model Upogalle.

2. Various products from QUASAR. On this page, Stratos. On the following, top, left and bottom, right, the model Boogie Woogie. Top, Cha, cha, cha. Bottom, Cube (left), all from QUASAR.

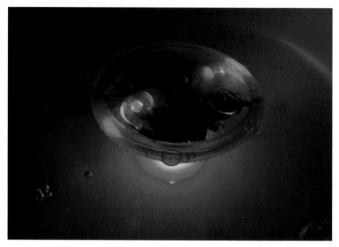

JEANNETTE ALTHERR

Jeannette Altherr was born in Heidelberg (Germany) in 1965. She studied at the School of Industrial Design of Darmstadt and later at the Massana School of Barcelona. Having completed her studies, she started work as a freelance designer and collaborated on various specialized publications and specifically on the EL PAIS weekly color supplement. In 1989, she started to work with Alberto Lievore. As fruit of this collaboration, the Lievore Altherr Molina studio came into being two years later. The company undertakes work in various areas of design and is particularly specialized in seating. Altherr is jointly responsible for design, consulting and art direction. The creator sees her work as a process that entails "observing, understanding, exploring, choosing, doubting, decision making, visualizing, letting go and hoping to communicate... something". She is the author of "Children Only", a book about objects and spaces for children edited by Carles Broto and which has been translated into various languages.

Profile

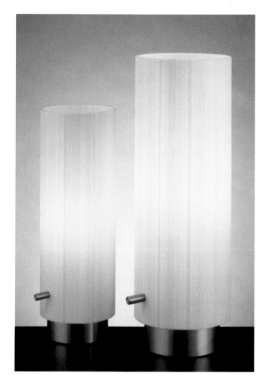

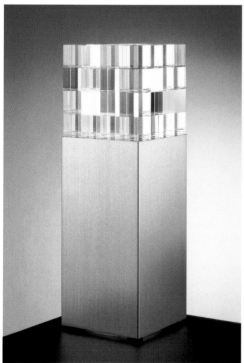

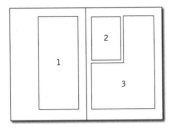

1. ALBUM produce the model Placid.

2. Zia Clara is another proposal from MURANODUE of the FIRME DI VETRO group.

3. Also from the brand ALBUM, the lamp Zorro (bottom) and Aba (top).

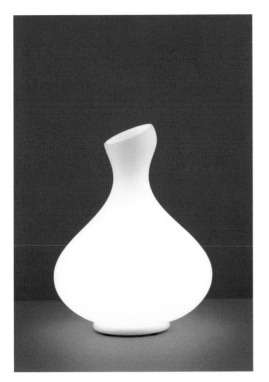

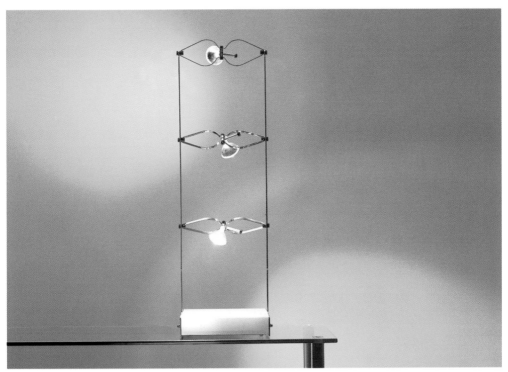

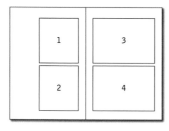

| 1 | 3 |
| 2 | 4 |

1. Turn on is a product from the brand ANN-UIT created by Marc Th. Van der Voorn.

2. Ross Lovegrove designed this seat lamp commercialized by BD.

3. A lamp from PREALPI.

4. A composition from ZANOTTA.

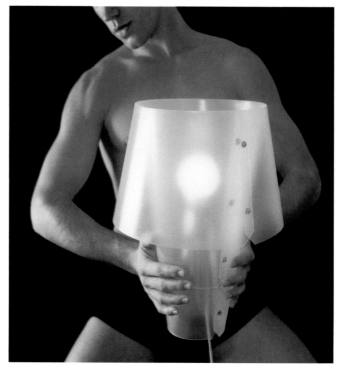

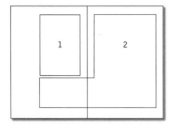

1. From KYOUEI CO ITD a design by Bekkou (Kouichi Okamoto), the Color Light dvd, which allows the color of the shade to be changed.

2. A version of the model Pascià from the collection New Classic by PENTA, designed by Gaia Bellavia. Bottom, Noa, by Massimo Belloni from the same brand.

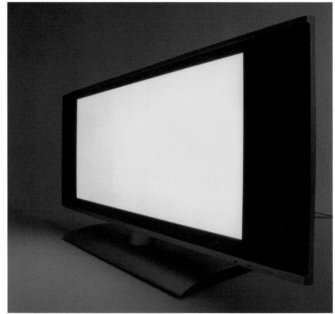

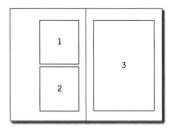

1. Aziz Sariyer designed the model Ice commercialized by DERIN.

2. MOBLES 114 BARCELONA propose this design by Massana and Tremoleda: Fil.

3. A table lamp from the DIEMO ALFONS catalog.

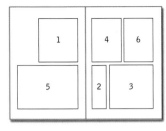

1. The table lamp Yu is a product from KUNDALINI which was designed by Marzio Rusconi Clerici.

2. A design by C+B Lefebvre for LIGNE ROSET, Two Watt.

3. Ingo Maurer and Team 2001 created Max Kluger, a lamp included in the INGO MAURER catalog.

4. A proposal that we can find in VINÇON stores, the table lamp T.

5. Crystal is a design from Dumoffice 9Dumoffice, produced by C-LECTION®. This model is made in Corian® Cameo White.

6. Valerio Bottin created Totem for FOSCARINI.

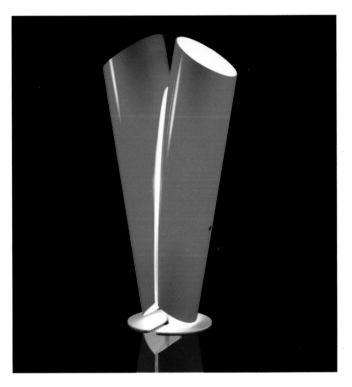

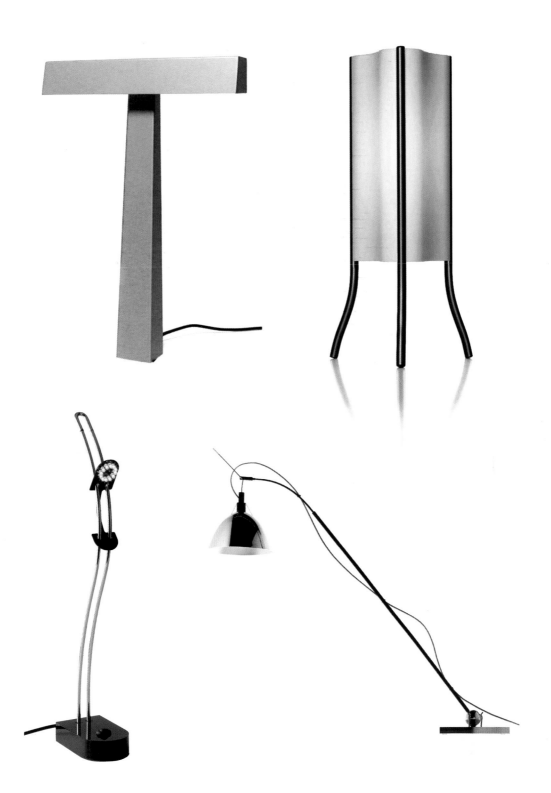

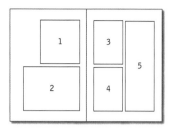

1. LIGNE ROSET include this design by Philippe Daney, Dolmen, in their catalog.

2. AAN_UIT commercialize the model Oog A.

3. Marco Zanuso designed Minimal for FONTANA ARTE.

4. ARTEK present Nueve.

5. Beppu (top) and Arima (bottom) from the firm SAWAYA & MORONI.

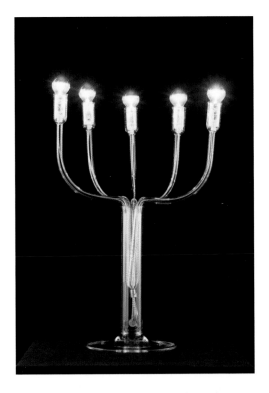

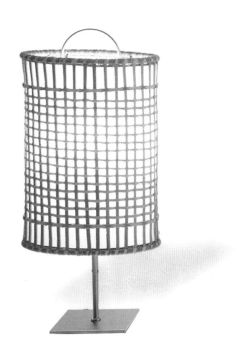

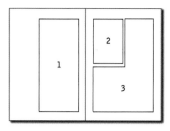

1. QUASAR commercialize the models: Moon (Top) Silver Spring (Bottom).

2. Also from the brand QUASAR, the model Empire State.

3. Wave (top and bottom, left) and Mujay (right), made in Murano glass, are other products from QUASAR.

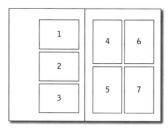

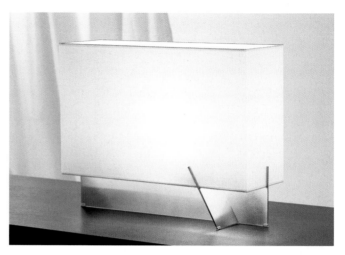

1. CARPYEN produce the model Nairobi by Gabriel Teixidó.

2. Radia Base is a product from the PALLUCO catalog.

3. Another proposal from MURANO DUE of the FIRME DI VETRO group: Paralume.

4. Dos is a model from the brand ARTEK.

5. Massimo Scolari designed this lamp for GIORGETTI.

6. FITZ LICHT present this model of table lamp.

7. Another creation by Gabriel Teixidó for CARPYEN: Aura.

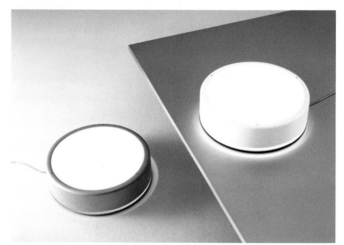

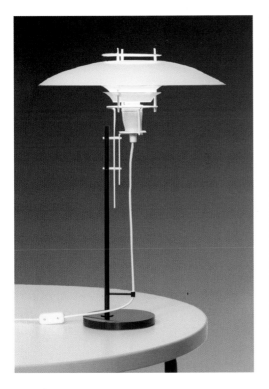

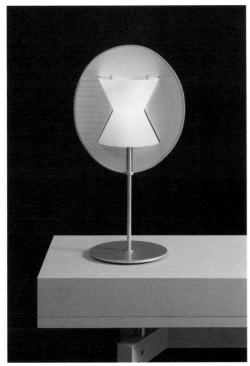

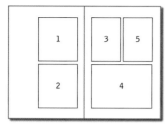

1. ALT LUCIALTERNATIVE (FIR-
   ME DI VETRO) produce the model Oriente.

2. A table lamp from VIABIZZU-
   NO.

3. Tutù is a design from Valerio Bottin, produced by FOSCARINI.

4. A proposal from MOONLIGHT
   for tabletops.

5. Pascual Salvador is the creator of
   the lamp Gilda commercialized by
   the company CARPYEN.

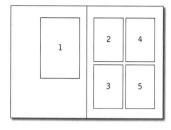

1. Soon is a proposal from TOBIAS GRAU.

2. Gregorio Spini created Notech for KUNDALINI.

3. Table lamp Angolo from the brand IGUZZINI.

4. Model Bill from TOBIAS GRAU.

5. Tolomeo Flu was created by Michele De Lucchi and Giancarlo Fassina for ARTEMIDE.

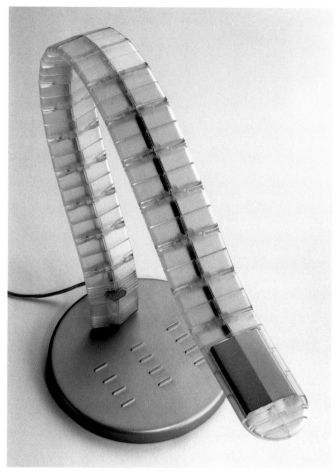

Profile

TOM DIXON

Tom Dixon is completely self-taught. He started in the design world by creating sculptural objects for pure pleasure until he realized that people were buying them and that "he could convert a pile of scrap into gold". His pieces started to obtain recognition and to be exhibited and he started to develop an interest in technology and industrial production. At the end of the 1980's, his international reputation was growing and Cappellini got in touch with him. This period is considered to be "his wilder creative period" and it is the time in which he produced the S-Chair which has become an icon and occupies a place in the permanent collection of the Museum of Modern Art in New York. One of his main preoccupations has always been that design should be attainable and, for this reason, he created Space in 1994 and has collaborated with Habitat since 1998.

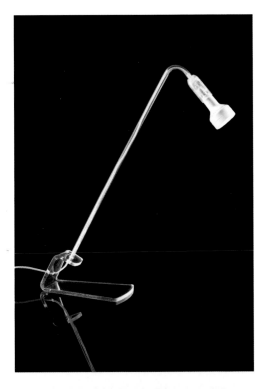

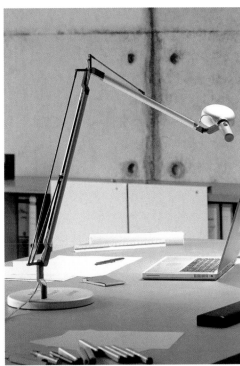

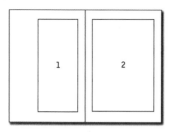

| 1 | 2 |

1. TECTA commercialize this design by George Carwardine, converted in a classic: Anglepoise. Top, one of the original packing cases from their first years of production.

2. FONTANA ARTE propose the model Ratio, created by Peter Christian.

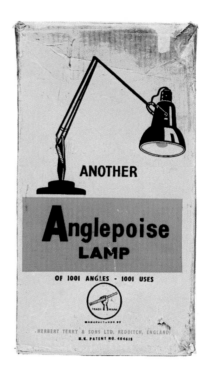

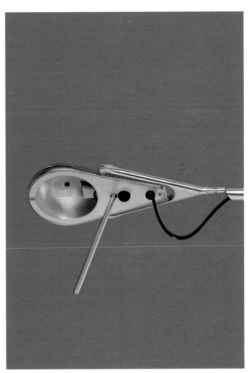
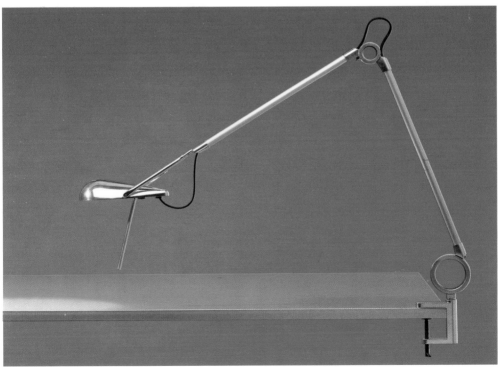

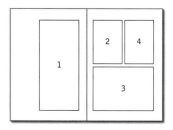

1. Aladina (top), Master (centro) and Galilea (bottom) are products from CARPYEN.

2. Kandido Tabolo is a model from the brand LUCITALIA.

3. Another proposal from INGO MAURER for illuminating the work table.

4. VINÇON propose this model from MOBLES 114: Giraplata.

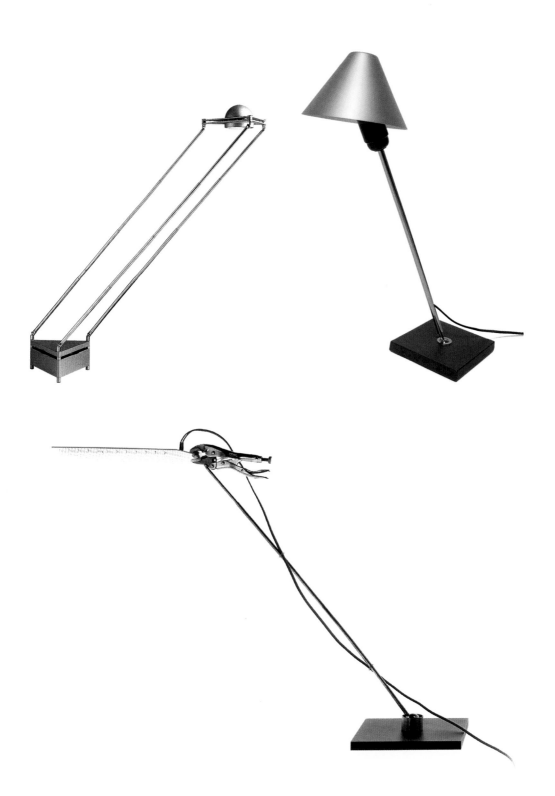

wall lamps

Wall lamps are frequently used to illuminate transit areas such as passages, halls and landings. They are also the eternal companions of bathroom mirrors. These fixtures tend to give off a strong beam of light although there are those that simply offer a touch of light to accentuate a particular point of interest be it a painting or a piece of decoration or those used to complete the overall illumination. There are even those that constitute a complement in themselves as many of the new proposals from the Swedish designers (ZLAMP). It is all about indirect illumination that is being extended more and more to areas in which standard lamps have traditionally been used.

In this section, we will see everything from the traditional wall lamps with a light beam that can be spread out evenly in all directions, or, if desired, upwards or downwards to the most imaginative proposals such as Lifelight from the Metalab collection from META-LARTE. For more contemporary and younger atmospheres, we will also see wall lamps with shades which enter into a play on colors and which not only contribute to creating very special atmospheres, but that influence in our moods and transmit different sensations to us according to the range of colors used.

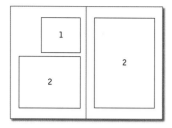

1. ELMAR FLÖTOTTO include these colored wall fittings in their catalog, Light Up 3.

2. Wall Tile with remote control (below these lines) and Sport Reflector Mixed (right) are two products from TRAXON.

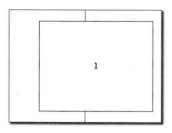

1. PALLUCO produce LaLinea, illumination combined with furniture. On these pages, various versions of this product designed by Andrea Marcante.

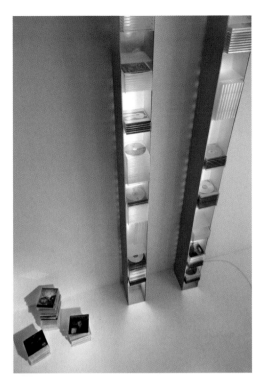

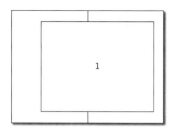

1. The design of LaLinea from the brand PALLUCO not only adapts to present-day decoration, but it is functional and elegant as well.

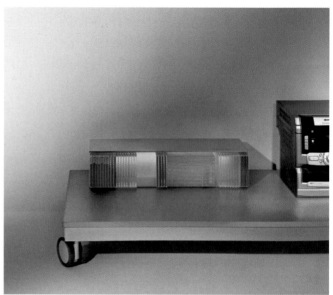

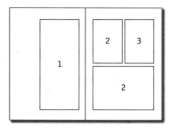

1. Magic Eyes is a wall fitting from the INGO MAURER catalog.

2. Ampelmann from OLIGO is also found as a wall fitting.

3. Kazuhiro Yamanaka created Rainy Day for PALLUCO.

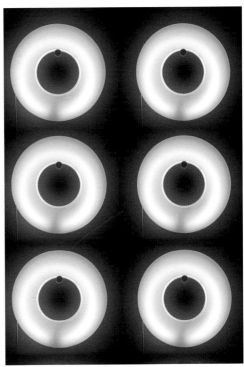

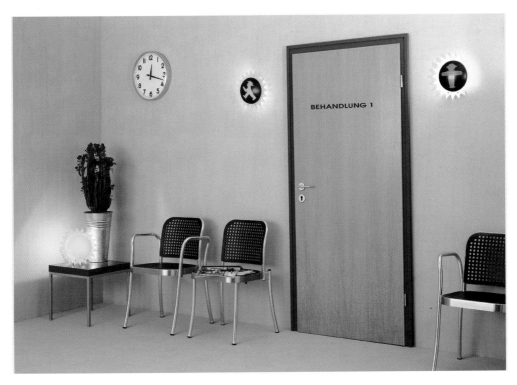

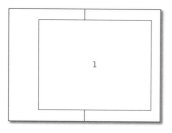

1. An exhibition of lamps from INGO MAURER in the VITRA DE-SIGN MUSEUM (next to these lines). Bottom and on the following page, another exhibition in Toronto.

Only lights 243 WALL LAMPS

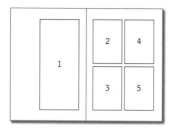

1. A product from VIABIZZUNO.

2. LUCEPLAN produce this versatile creation by Eduard François:
   Rosaverde.

3. Kub by Mark Frost is a proposal
   from IDL.

4. Also from VIABIZZUNO, Bamboo.

5. From the ARTEMIDE catalog,
   the model K I I I.

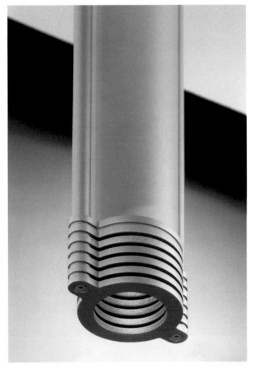

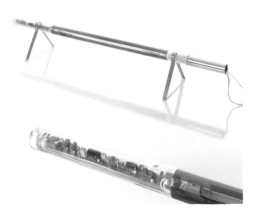

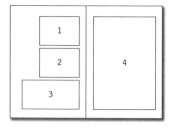

1. A design from INGO MAURER.
2. Cypress is a wall fitting from the brand QUASAR.
3. LLEDÓ ILUMINACIÓN propose the model LEDS OB-4570 (left) and LEDS OB-4550 (right).
4. Other designs from INGO MAURER.

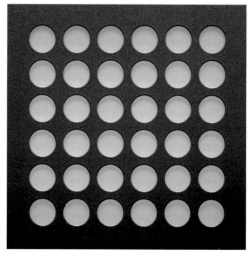

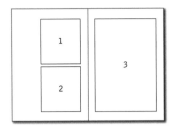

1. PREALPI propose this wall lamp.

2. Lucellin is another creation from INGO MAURER.

3. Different products from VIABIZ-ZUNO.

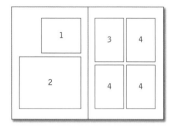

1. Smoke is a product from DAB, designed by David Abad.

2. Ross Lovegrove designed the wall lamp Google for LUCEPLAN.

3. DAB also propose Leds Screen.

4. FOSCARINI include the models Maui (bottom, Left) and Flat by Piero Lissoni (top, right) in their catalog. Bottom, Bit by Ferruccio Laviani from the same brand.

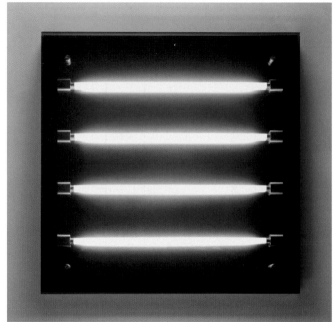

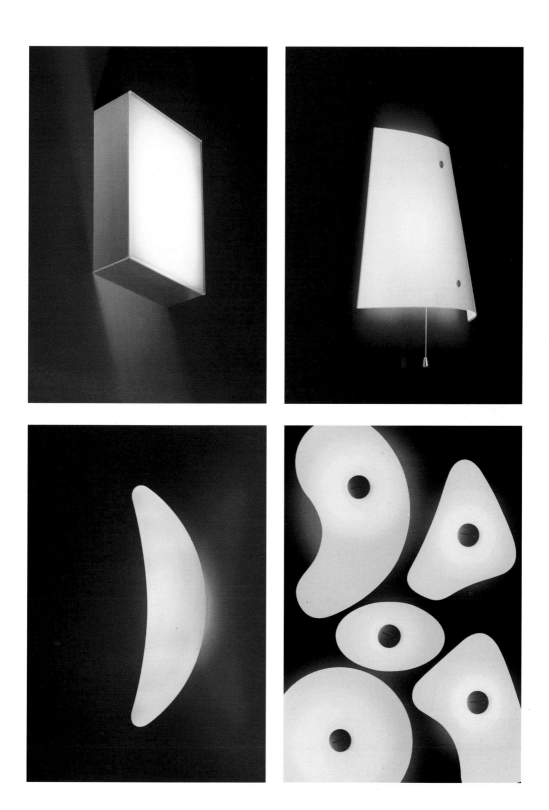

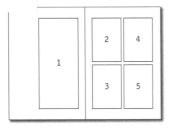

1. Liana (Top) is a wall lamp from AQUA CREATIONS. SameSame (bottom, left) and Contrare Cream (on the right) are other creations from the "Light of My Life" catalog characterized by organic forms.

2. SLD (Scandinavian Lamp Design) propose this wall lamp from the collection "Made in Småland", Heart, from the brand SKRUF. It is a design from Björn Hultqvist

3. B.LUX - VANLUX present Sare.

4. ARTEMIDE produce Go to the Mirror.

5. Magic from ILLU STRATION.

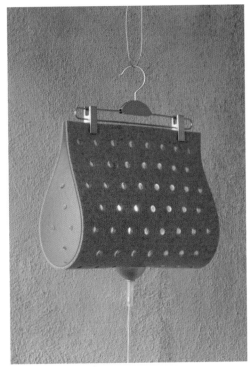

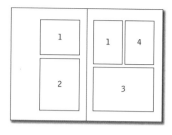

1. Hip Hop from ILLU STRATION, designed by Alexander Pernitschka and Mary-Ann Williams.

2. From the Metalab collection by METALARTE, Lifelight, a creation from Jordi Llopis.

3. FOSCARINI produce Yet, a design from Studio Karos.

4. Cheyenne is a wall lamp from ESSENTIA.

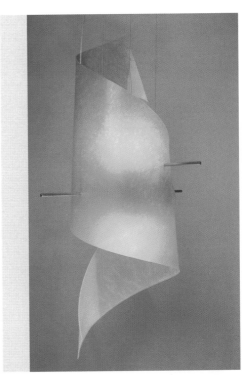

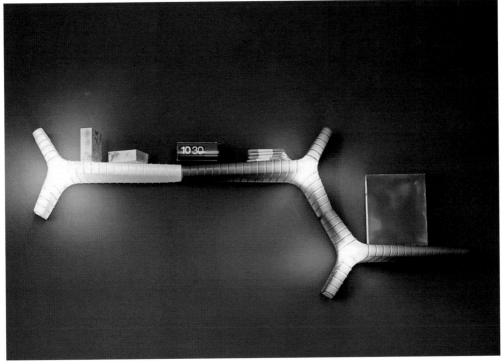

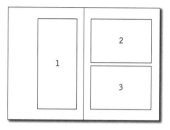

1. DELTALIGHT produce Connect (top) and Be Cool (bottom).

2. O Lite is a wall lamp proposed by ANSORG & BELUX for the bathroom.

3. DELTALIGH include Tubular DS in their catalog.

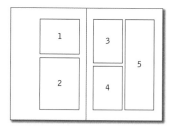

1. A design by Joan Gaspar for MARSET: Neon Luz.

2. FIRME DI VETRO propose Rockette 58 from the ITRE catalog.

3. Relax is a product from FONTANA ARTE.

4. PALLUCOITALIA present Tube.

5. Light Up 1 (top) and Light Up 2 (bottom) are two models from ELMAR FLÖTOTTO.

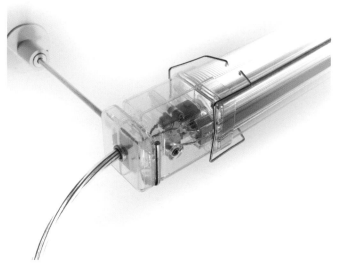

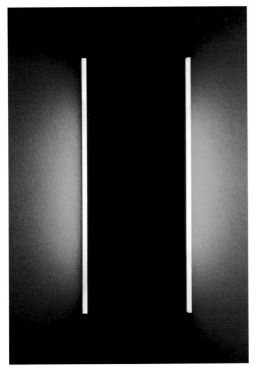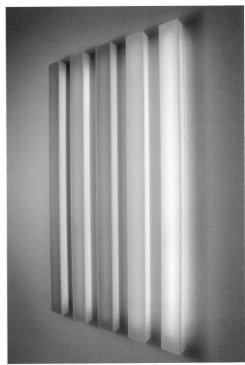
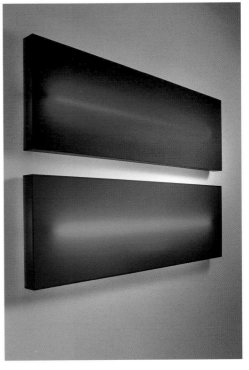

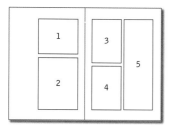

1. Big Round is a model from EL-MAR FLÖTOTO.

2. Quadra 35 is another proposal from FIRME DI VETRO from the brand MURANODUE.

3. FOSCARINI produce Ellepi by Alessandra Matilde.

4. Vision is a wall lamp from ILLU STRATION.

5. Johanna Hitzler designed the Kleine Lampe orange (top) and Kleine Lampe Rund (bottom).

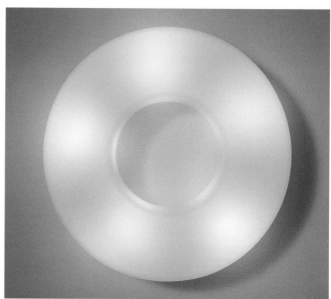

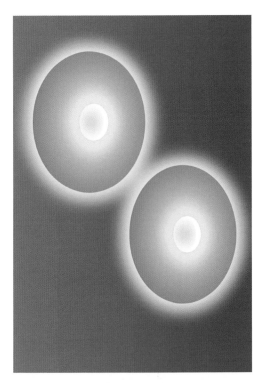

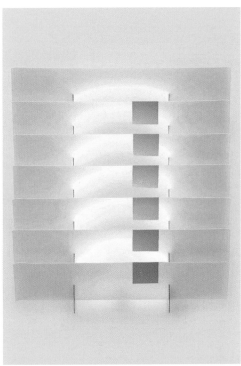

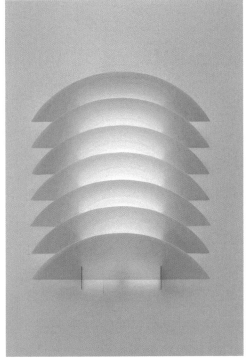

exterior lamps

In this section, a series of lamps designed for the exterior have been brought together. The fact that they are for the outside and must therefore be resistant to weather conditions has dictated the use of materials to a large extent. They may be exposed to the sun for lengthy periods of time during the day, to the humidity of the night and early morning, to the cold of winter and to the summer heat. They generally tend to be lamps that are more centered on their functional aspect and of a more minimalist conception to blend in with contemporary styles of architecture. Durability is another fundamental aspect although we will also find some of a great beauty in which design is of equal importance. In this section, we will find lights to illuminate accesses, drives, paths or entrances and different areas of the garden. There are also waterproof lights that can be floated in swimming pools or ponds. We will see that the imagination that has been let loose in this section has manifested itself in the form of color and organic forms that appear in the landscape like full moons or little mountains of light. Color is one of the latest tendencies that have been introduced into this area generally dominated by metallic and matt finishes and the use of glass in the lampshades.

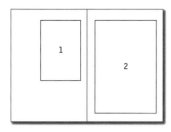

1. Blob M is a proposal for the exterior designed by Karim Rashid and from the brand FOSCARINI.

2. MOONLIGHT suggest this model for exteriors.

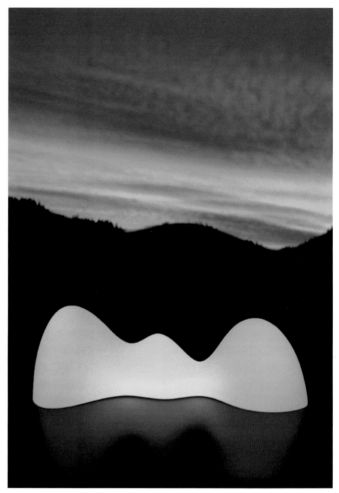

KARIM RASHID

This prolific designer was born in Cairo (1960), of Canadian nationality, is an arduous defender of democratic design. He is convinced that a good creation should not be elitist, but that it should be within the reach of everybody in the world. A clear example of how he puts this philosophy into practice is the garbage bucket Garbo, in polypropylene, of which he has sold more than two million examples in the USA. It is used by some as a champagne bucket and has been included in the collection of the Museum of San Francisco. The adjective that would best define his work is, without a doubt, organic: of sinuous forms, with rounded corners and sensuous so that the interaction between persons and objects are of an agreeable experience. Rashid finds his inspiration in natural forms. His fundamental tools are computer science and the new technologies.

Profile

>>

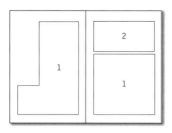

1. Different products from the catalog MOONLIGHT that stand out for their versatility.

2. METALARTE present this waterproof and rechargeable exterior lamp made in molded polyethylene from the Metalab collection. Waterproofs is a design from Héctor Serrano.

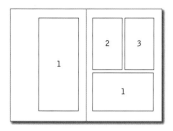

1. From the MOONLIGHT catalog, different lamps in various colors and sizes for interior and exterior use.

2. Blob XL, commercialized by FOSCARINI.

3. Arata Isozaki is the creator of this model, Signoria, produced by ARTEMIDE.

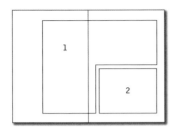

1. Alongside these lines, the models
   Wega (top) and Wisdom (bottom
   and top, on the following page)
   from KISS.

1. Various models from the firm
   KISS.

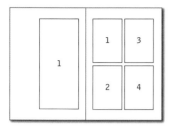

1. Focus System, designed by Foster & Partners (on this page) and RL V (on the following) are models from the brand ARTEMIDE for the exterior.

2. DAB propose Blok Outdoor, in two different sizes.

3. A lamppost model proposed by MOONLIGHT.

4. Night Light in different sizes. A product from the firm CONMO-TO.

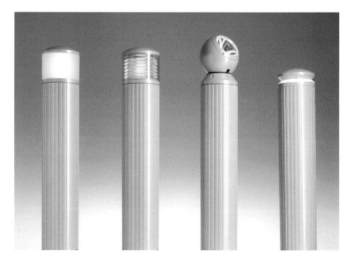

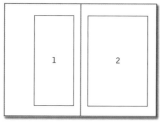

1. Little Big Lamp is a lamp from INGO MAURER.

2. IPJ distribute this model for the interior and exterior from the brand BERND BEISSE.

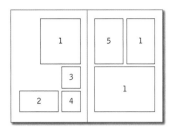

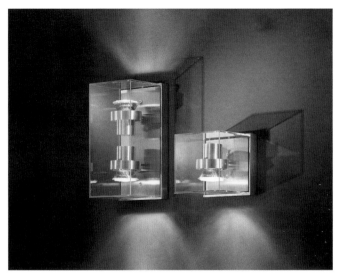

1. ILUMINACIÓN PETER JAHN propose these models from the brand IP44. On this page, Annton. On the following page, bottom, left, Hoch. On the right, Bild.

2. From the DELTALIGHT catalog, from left to right: top, Polaris Red and Radar; bottom, the Sonar 10 A and the Sonar 15 Steak.

3. LLEDÓ ILUMINACIÓN propose the model LEDS OB-4521.

4. Model RL V from ARTEMIDE.

5. Light Up Walk is a product from the brand IGUZZINI for the exterior.

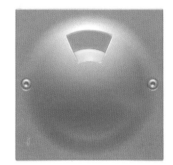

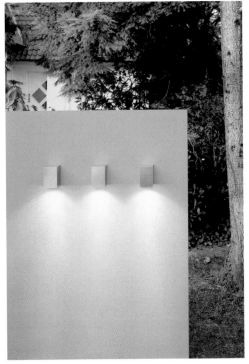

1. Various proposals from ILUMI-NACIÓN PETER JAHN, from the brand IP44. Alongside these lines, the model Paca.

>>

Profile

ROSS LOVEGROVE

Lovegrove is one of the international designers who is enjoying a high level of personal prestige on the present international panorama. He was born in Cardiff (Wales) in 1958. At the beginning of the 1980's, he worked for Frog Design in Germany. Later, he moved to Paris and became assessor to Knoll International and obtained great success thanks to the Alessandri Office System. He joined Atelier in Nimes along with Jean Nouvel and Philippe Starck where he took on the responsibility for advising, among other, Cacharel Louis Vuitton, Hermes and Dupont. In 1988, he moved to London and set out upon a number of projects for companies such as Kartell, Cappellini or Luceplan. Lovegrove's products are innovative. They are full of vitality and daring. His curiosity and his passion for materials and production processes are some of the fundamental elements of this designer's creations and aspects that give them a particular singularity.

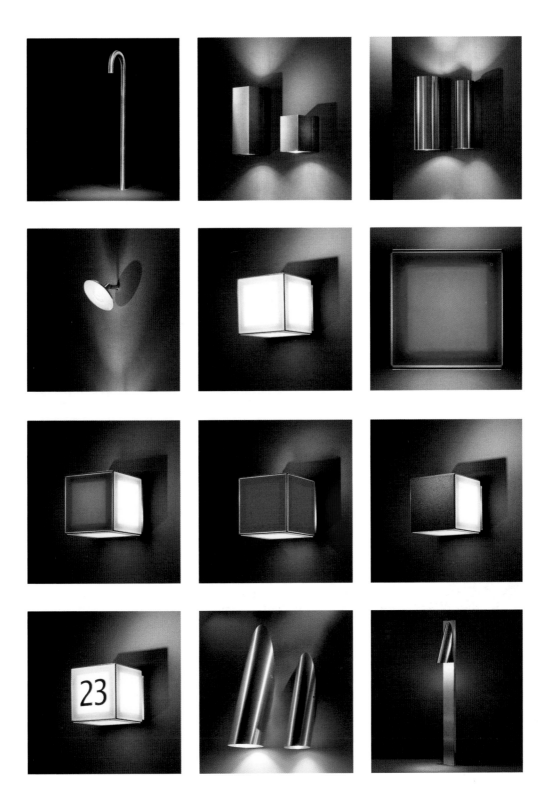

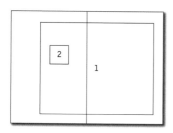

1. Various models offered by ILU-MINACIÓN PETER JAHN from the brand IP44.

2. Fuser is a wall lamp for the exterior from MODULAR LIGHTING INSTRUMENTS.

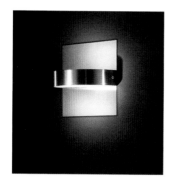

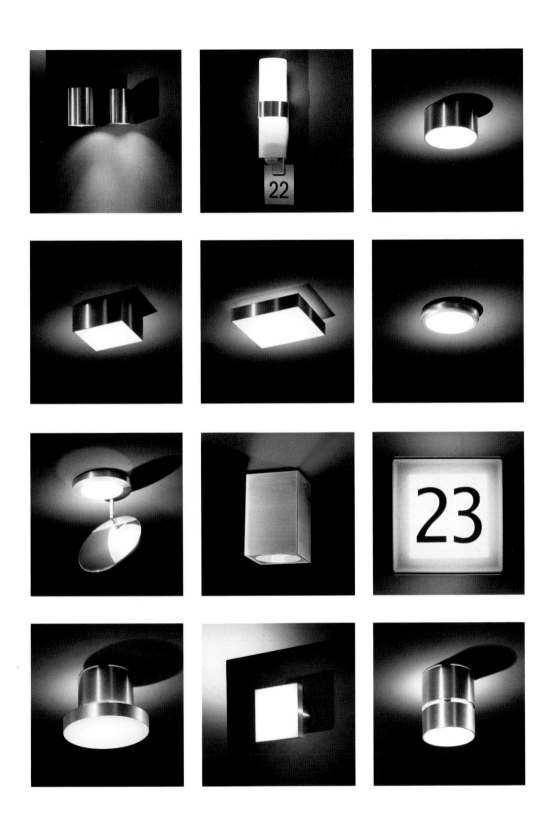

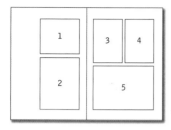

1. ALT LUCIALTERNATIVE (FIR-
   ME DI VETRO) produce this model for the garden in different
   heights and colors: Omega PL40
   Garden.

2. MODULAR LIGHTING INS-
   TRUMENTS present the lamp
   Kabaz.

3. Oval is a product for the exterior
   commercialized by CARPYEN.

4. Fanco Raggi designed this model
   for ARTEMIDE: Verdeluce.

5. Bridge from the brand DELTA-
   LIGHT.

directory

ALBUM LIGHTING (See NEX VERSUS for agent in SPAIN)
Via Cavallotti 19
20046 Biassono (Milano)
ITALY
Tel. 39 039 220 041
Fax. 39 0 392 200 444
album@album.it
www.album.it

ANSORG-BELUX
Solinger Str. 19
45481 Mülheim a. d. Ruhr
GERMANY
Tel. 49 2 084 840
Fax,. 49 020 848 461 200
info@ansorg.com
www.ansorg.com
www.belux.com

ANTHOLOGIE QUARTET
Schloss Hünnenfeld
49152 Bad Essen
GERMANY
Tel. 49 0 547 294 090
Fax. 49 05 472 940 940
info@anthologiequartett.de
www.anthologiequartett.de

AQUA CREATIONS
69 Mazeh St.
65789 Tel Aviv
ISRAEL
Tel. 97 235 602 197
Fax. 97 235 607 756
israel@aquagallery.com

AQUA CREATIONS USA
200 Lexington Avenue. Between 32nd and 33rd St.
Suite 436
N.Y 10016 New York
U.S.A.
Tel. 2122 199 922
Fax. 2 122 194 042
USA@aquagallery.com

www.aquagallery.com

ARCAYA EQUIP (Distributed in SPAIN by: VIABIZZUNO)
San Martín, 1 Bajo Trasera

01130 Álava
SPAIN
Tel. 34 945 462 408
Fax. 34 945 462 446
arcaya@jet.es

ARRMET
Z.i. Via A.Volta, s/n
33044 Manzano (UD)
ITALY
Tel. 39 0 432 937 065/6/7
Fax. 39 0 432 740 102
mail@arrmet.it
www.arrmet.it

ARTEK
Eteläesplanadi 18
00130 Helsinki
FINLAND
Tel. 358 961 325 277
Fax. 358 961 325 265
info@artek.fi
www.artek.fi

ARTEK representatives USA

Baldinger Lighting
19-02 Steinway St.
Astoria, NY 11105
U.S.A.
Tel. 17 182 045 700
Fax. 17 187 214 986
www.baldingerlighting.com

ARTEMIDE ITALIA
Via Bergamo 18
20010 Pregnana Milanese (MI)
Tel. 39 02 93518.1 – 93526.1
Fax. 02 93 590 254 – 93 590 496
info@artemide.com
www.artemide.com

ARTEMIDE in SPAIN
C/Lérida 68-70
08820 Prat de Llobregat (Barcelona)
SPAIN
Tel. 34 934 783 911
Fax. 34 933 707 306
artemide@artemide.e.telefonica.net
www.artemide.com

AVANTUM (distribute in SPAIN and PORTUGAL: SKANDINAVISK LAMP DESIGN – SLD.)
info@avantum.info
www.avantum.info

BALD AND BANGS (Distribution and sale by IQL LIGHT)

-Rosenoernsalle 39
baghuset, st
1970 Frederiksberg C
DENMARK
Tel. 45 33 360 776
Fax. 45 70 213 030
Sole distributors: r.elmin@bald-bang.com

-Laederstraeade 36
1201 Copenhagen K
DENMARK
Tel. 45 33 360 776
sales@iqlight.com
www.bald-bang.com

BD
C/Mallorca 291
08037 Barcelona
SPAIN
Tel. 34 934 586 909
Fax. 34 932 073 697
www.bdbarcelona.com
www.bdediciones.com

BELUX in SWITZERLAND:

-Klünenfeldstrasse 20
CH-4127 Birsfelden
SWITZERLAND
Tel. 41 613 167 401
Fax. 41 613 167 599

-Bremgarterstrasse 109
CH-5610 Wohlen
SWITZERLAND
Tel. 41 566 18 7 373
Fax. 41 566 187 327

belux@belux.com
www.belux.com

BELUX in SPAIN:

-BELUX SPAIN
Pza. Comercial, 4
08003 Barcelona
SPAIN

Tel. 34 932 688 705
Fax. 34 932 688 706
spain@belux.com

-Polígono Eitua, 70
48240 Berriz
SPAIN
Tel. 34 946 827 272
Fax. 34 946 824 902
info@grupoblux.com

B.LUX, S.A. (Factory)
Okamika Ind. Pab. 1,
48289 Guizaburuaga,
Tel. 34 946 842 950
Fax. 34 946 243 699

CARPYEN
Pere IV, 78-84
08005 Barcelona
SPAIN
Tel. 34 933 209 990
Fax. 34 933 209 991
comercial@carpyen.com
www.carpyen.com

CATTELAN ITALIA
Via Pilastri 15
36010 Carré (VI)
ITALY
Tel. 39 04 453 187 711
Fax. 39 0 445 314 289
info@cattelanitalia.com
www.cattelanitalia.com

CLASSICON
Sigmund-Riefler-Bogen 3
81829 München
GERMANY
Tel. 49 897 481 330
Fax. 49 897 809 996
info@classicon.com
www.classicon.com

C-LECTION

Kievitstraat 4
5262 ZD Vught
THE NETHERLANDS
info@clection.com
www.clection.com

CONMOTO
Schloß Möhler,
Schloßallee 6
33442 Herzebrock-Clarholz
GERMANY
Tel. 49 5 245 921 920
Fax. 49 52 459 219 222
Info@conmoto.com
www.conmoto.com

DAB (DISEÑO ACTUAL BARCE-
LONA)
Avda. de la Cerdanya, Nau 10
Pol. Ind Pomar de Dalt
08915 Badalona (Barcelona)
SPAIN
Tel. 34 934 650 818
Fax. 34 934 654 635
info@dab.es
www.dab.es

DELTA LIGHT
Industrieweg 72
8800 Roeselare
BELGIUM
Tel. 32 051 272 627
Fax. 32 051 210 483
promotion@deltalight.com
www.deltalight.com

DEPADOVA
Corso Venezia 14
20121 Milano
ITALY
Tel. 39 02 777 201
Fax. 39 0 277 720 280
clienti@depadova.it
www.depadova.it

DERIN DESIGN
Abdj Ipekçl Caddesl, 77/1
Maçka, Istambul
TURKEY
Tel. 902 122 252 003
Fax. 902 122 251 955
info@derindesign.com

www.derindesign.com

DIEMO ALFONS
Rosenthaler Str. 19
10119 Berlín
GERMANY
Tel. 49 308 522 975
Fax. 49 3 085 964 353
info@diemo-alfons.de
www.diemo-alfons.de

ELITE
Viale Trento, 59/A
33077 Sacile (PN)
ITALY
Tel. 39 0 434 738 092
Fax. 39 0 434 781 057
info@elite-srl.it
www.elite-srl.it

ELMAR FLÖTOTTO
Am Ölbach 28
33334 Gütersloh
GERMANY
Tel. 49 0 524 194 050
Fax. 49 052 419 405 250
verkauf@elmarfloetotto.de
www.elmarfloetotto.de

FIRME DI VETRO (ITRE, MURA-
NODUE, AURELIANO TOSO, ALT
LUCIALTERNATIVE, GALLERY)
Via delle Industrie 16/c
30030 Salzano (VE)
ITALY
Tel. 39 0 415 741 111
Fax. 39 041 482 691
info@firmedivetro.com
www.firmedivetro.com

FONTANAARTE
Alzaia Trieste, 49
20094 Corsico (Mi)
ITALY
Tel. 39 0 245 121
Fax. 39 024 512 660
info@fontanaarte.it
www.fontanaarte.it

FOSCARINI
Via delle Industrie 27
30020 Marcon (Ve)
ITALY
Tel. 39 0 415 953 811
Fax. 39 04 115 959 232
foscarini@foscarini.com
www.foscarini.it

GIORGETTI
Via Manzoni, 20
20036 Meda (MI)
ITALY
Tel. 39 036 275 275
Fax. 39 036 275 575
giorspa@giorgetti-spa.it
www.giorgetti-spa.it

GREEN
Via Torino
56010 Vicopisano (PI)
ITALY
Tel. 39 50 796 152
Fax. 39 50 796 987
info@greensrl.it
www.greensrl.it

HK – HANS KAUFELD
Grafenheider Straße 20
33729 Bielefeld
GERMANY
info@hans-kaufeld.com
www.hans-kaufeld.com

IDL – LEUCHTEN
Annaberger Straße 73
09111 Chemnitz
GERMANY
Tel. 49 0 372 263 100
Fax. 49 0 372 287 112
info@idl-leuchten.de
www.idl-leuchten.de

IGUZZINI
S.S.77, Km 102
62019 Recanati (MC)
ITALY
Tel. 39 07 175 881
iguzzini@iguzzini.it
www.iguzzini.com

IGUZZINI ILUMINAZIONE ES-

PAÑA S.A.
Polígono Industrial Can Jardí,
C/ Strauss, s/n
08191 Rubí (Barcelona)
SPAIN
Tel. 34 935 880 034
Fax. 34 936 999 974
iguzzini@iguzzini.es
www.iguzzini.es

ILLU STRATION
Schulstr. 3-5
63849 Leidersbach
Tel. 49 6 028 993 898
illustration@directbox.com
www.illustration.de.tt

INGO MAURER GmbH
Kaiserstrasse 47
80801 München
GERMANY
Tel. 49 893 816 06 – 0
Fax: 49 893 81 606 20
info@ingo-maurer.com

INGO MAURER LLC
89 Grand Street
New York, NY 10013
U.S.A.
Tel. 2 129 658 817
Fax. 2 129 658 819
making-light@ingomaurer.usa.com

www.ingo-maurer.com

IPJ LUZ - ILUMINACIÓN PETER
JAHN (Distributed by AXELMEI-
SELICHT, BERN BEISSE, IP44,
SCHMITZ-LEUCHTEN ITZ)
Grupo Escolar, 62
07620 Llucmajor (Baleares)
SPAIN
Tel. 34 971 120 999
Fax. 34 971 121 007
info@ipjluz.com
www.ipjluz.com

IQL LIGHT (See BALD AND
BAGS.)

JOHANNA HITZLER
Puschkinstrasse 22

06108 Halle
GERMANY
Tel. 49 03 452 908 506
johitzler@web.de

KARTELL S.a.P
Via delle industrie 1
20082 Noviglio (MI)
ITALY
Tel. 39 02 900 121
Fax. 39 0 290 091 212
kartell@kartell.it
www.kartell.it

KUNDALINI
Via F. De Sanctis, 34
20141 Milano
ITALY
Tel. 39 0 284 800 088
Fax. 39 0 284 800 096
info@kundalini.it
www.kundalini.it

KYOUEI CO
731 Shimizukitawaki Shizuoka City
Shizuoka
JAPAN
Tel. 81 543 470 654
Fax. 81 543 474 455
info@kyouei-ltd.co.jp
www.kyouei-ltd.co.jp

LOOKILUZ - APARTE DE MOBI-
LIARIO S.L
Àlaba, 129
08018 Barcelona
SPAIN
Tel. 34 933 208 370
Fax. 34 933 002 404
aparte@lookiluz.com
wwwlookiluz.com

L.I.N. (LINDNER IM NORDEN)
Wagnerstrasse 56a
22081 Hamburg
GERMANY
Tel. 49 0 40/55 773 770
Fax. 49 0 40/55 773 771
info@lindnerimnorden.com
www.lindnerimnorden.com

LUCEPLAN
Via E.T. Moneta 46
20161 Milano
ITALY
Tel. 39 02 662 421
Fax. 39 02 66 203 400
luceplan@luceplan.com
luceplanstore@luceplan.com
www.luceplan.com

MARSET
Alfonso XII 429-431
08918 Badalona
SPAIN
Tel. 34 934 602 067
Fax. 34 934 601 089
info@marset.com
www.marset.com

METALARTE (Showroom)
Tambor de Bruc, 10
08970 San Joan Despí (Barcelona)
SPAIN
Tel. 34 934 770 069
Fax. 34 93 477 00 86
metalarte@metalarte.com
www.metalarte.com

MOBILIFICIO PREALPI
Via Fossa 15
31051 Follina
ITALY
Tel. 39 0 438 970 277
info@prealpi.it
www.prealpi.it

MOBLES 114 BARCELONA
Riera dels Frares 24
08097 Hospitalet del Llobregat
(Barcelona)
SPAIN
Tel. 34 932 600 114
Fax. mobles114@mobles114.com
www.mobles114.com

MOONLIGHT – OSWALD
Gewerbegebiet Hemmet
79664 Wehr
GERMANY
Tel. 49 77 621 018
Fax. 49 77 622 203
info@moonlight.outdoorlighting.de

www.moonlight.outdoorlighting.de

NEX VERSUS (Agent in Spain for
ALBUM and PENTA)
Ángel Espinosa
C/ 106, n° 12
46182 La Canada (Valencia)
SPAIN
Tel. 34 961 325 051
Fax. 34 961 321 258
forum.internacional@infonegocio.com

OLIGO Lichttechnik GMBH
Meysstraße 22-24
53773 Hennef
GERMANY
Tel. 49 0 224 287 02-0
Fax. 49 02 242 870 2-88
info@oligo.de
www.oligo.de

PALLUCCO ITALIA - BELLATO
Via Azzi 36
31040 Castagnole di Paese Treviso
Tel. 0422 438 500
Fax. 0422 438955
infobellato@palluccobellato.it
www.palluccobellato.it

PENTA (See NEX VERSUS for
agent in SPAIN)
Via M.L. King, 8
22060 Cabiate (Co)
ITALY
Tel. 39 031 766 100
Fax. 39 031 756 102
info@pentalight.it
www.pentalight.it

QUASAR DESIGN HOLLAND
Burgstraat 2
4283 GG Giessen
THE NETHERLANDS
Tel. 31 183 447 887
Fax. 31 183 447 879
info@quasar.nl
www.itc-partners.com

ROLF BENZ
Haiterbacher Strasse 104

72202 Nagold
GERMANY
Tel. 49 7 452 601 245
Fax. 49 7 452 601 110
www.rolf-benz.de

RP - LAMPS (Alex Gabriel & Willeke Evenhuis)
Oude Velperweg 38
6824 HE Arnhem
THE NETHERLANDS
Tel. 31 263 894 536
alexgabriel@gmx.net
www.rp-lamps.com

SANTA & COLE
Santísima Trinidad del Monte 10
08017 Barcelona
SPAIN
Tel. 34 934 183 396
Fax. 34 934 183 812
www.santacole.com

SAWAYA & MORONI
Via Andegari, 18
20121 Milán
ITALY
Tel. 39 02 86 395.1
Fax. 39 02 86 39 5212 – 200
info@sawayamoroni.com
www.sawayamoroni.com

SCP FURNITURE
135-139 Curtain Road
EC2A 3BX London
UNITED KINGDOM
Tel. 44 0 2 077 391 869
Fax. 44 0 2 077 294 224
info@scp.co.uk
www.scp.co.uk

SKANDIUM
86 Marylebone High Street
W1U 4QS London
UNITED KINGDOM
Tel. 44 02 079 352 077
Fax. 44 02 079 352 099
info@skandium.com
www.skandium.com
www.marimekko.co.uk